AF342450

Chinese Festivals

Qi Xin

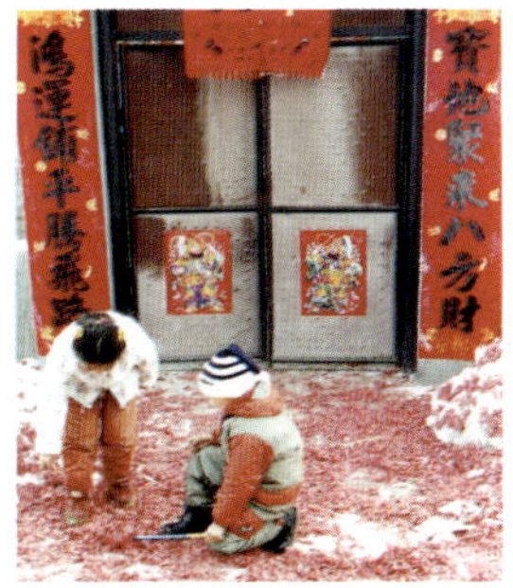

Foreign Languages Press

First Edition 2008

ISBN 978-7-119-05407-0
©Foreign Languages Press, Beijing, China, 2008
Published by Foreign Languages Press
24 Baiwanzhuang Road, Beijing 100037, China
http://www.flp.com.cn
Distributed by China International Book Trading Corporation
35 Chegongzhuang Xilu, Beijing 100044, China
P.O. Box 399, Beijing, China

Printed in the People's Republic of China

Festivals are markers of time, dividing the year into many periods. These periods constitute our lives and festivals are highlights in the course of our living. At festivals, people celebrate good harvests, pray for favorable weather for their crops, or try to fend off evil spirits in the hope of bringing tranquility to the home.

China has a long history of agriculture, so at their earliest stages its festivals were intimately tied up with farming. The calendar used in times gone by—the lunar calendar—was formulated in accordance with farming seasons, and, based on this calendar, people would plant in spring, plough in summer, harvest in fall and store their crops in winter. During breaks between the farming seasons, people would celebrate harvests and pray for good weather for the coming farming season. It was during this process that festivals came into being. Even now, traditional Chinese festivals are celebrated in accordance with the lunar calendar.

With the passage of time, the weather and farming elements of festivals gradually faded. Some festivals commemorate Chinese ancestors, for example the Dragon Boat Festival in memory of the ancient poet Qu Yuan; some have their origins in myth, such as the Seventh Night Festival—the night every year when Cowherd Boy and Weaver Maid were believed to meet in heaven; others are the results of religious beliefs, such as the Hungry Ghost Festival and the Laba Festival—both products of Buddhism. Behind each festival lies a legend in which the joys or sufferings experienced by the ancient Chinese people are remembered. Exploring traditional Chinese festivals is like opening a window to history, a window through which we can glimpse the lives of our ancestors.

Today, we Chinese continue to celebrate these festivals, bringing people even closer to their ancestors, creators of a splendid culture.

CONTENTS

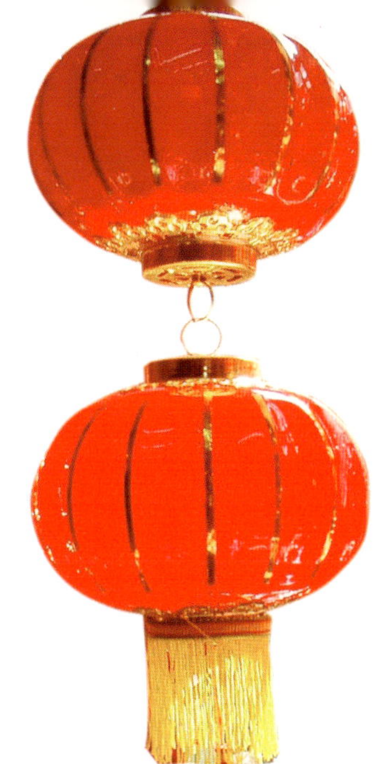

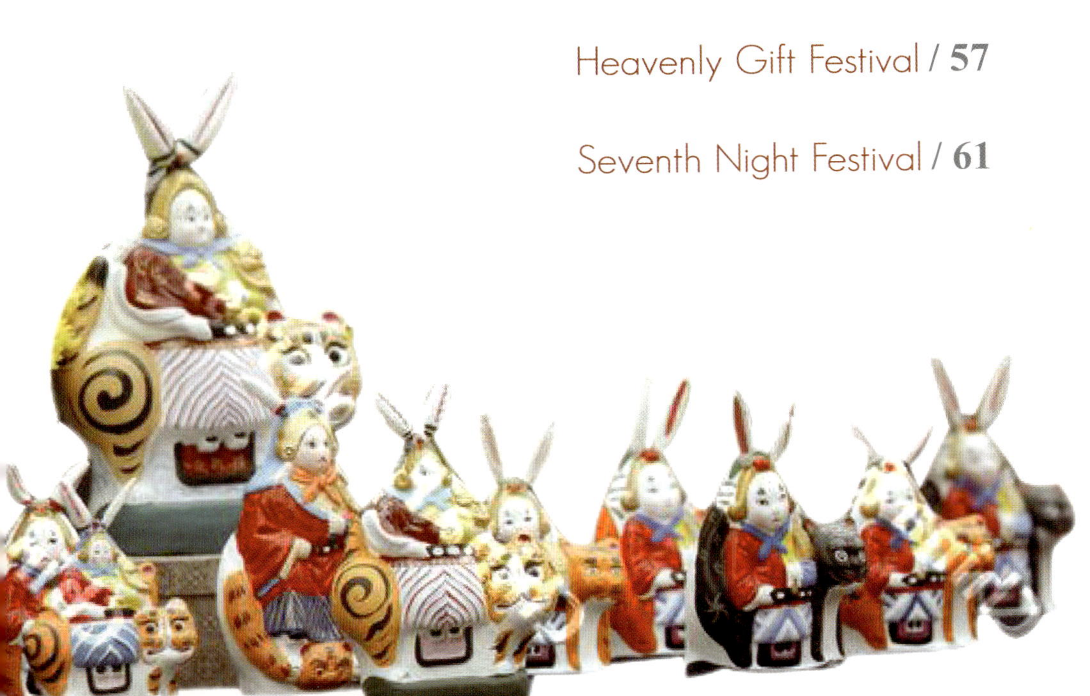

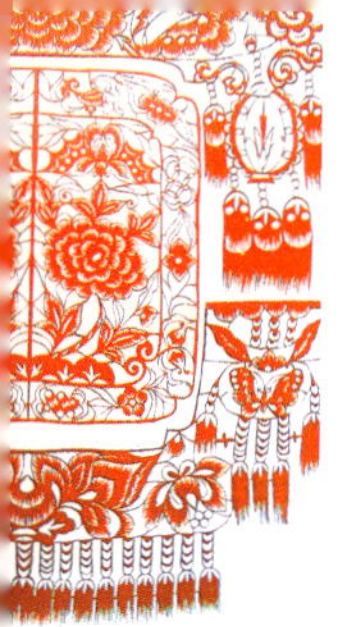

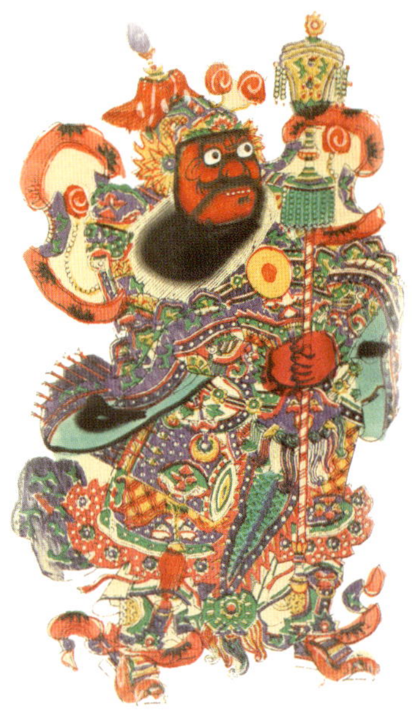

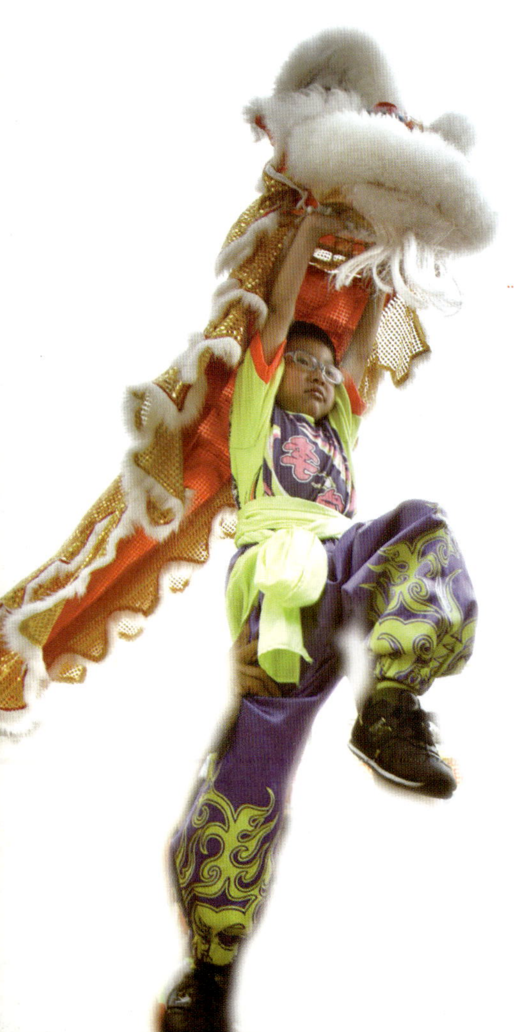

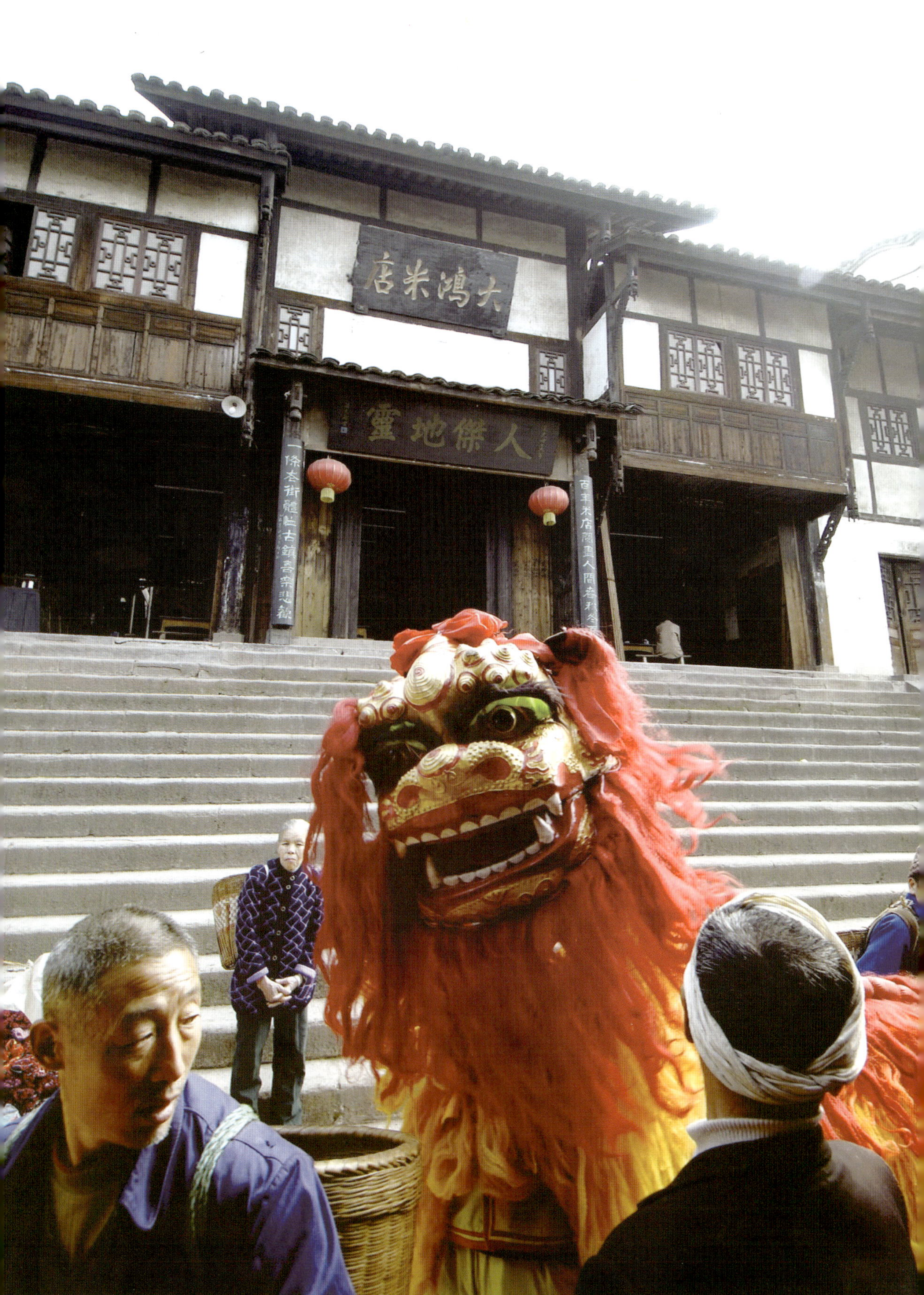
大鴻米店
人傑地靈

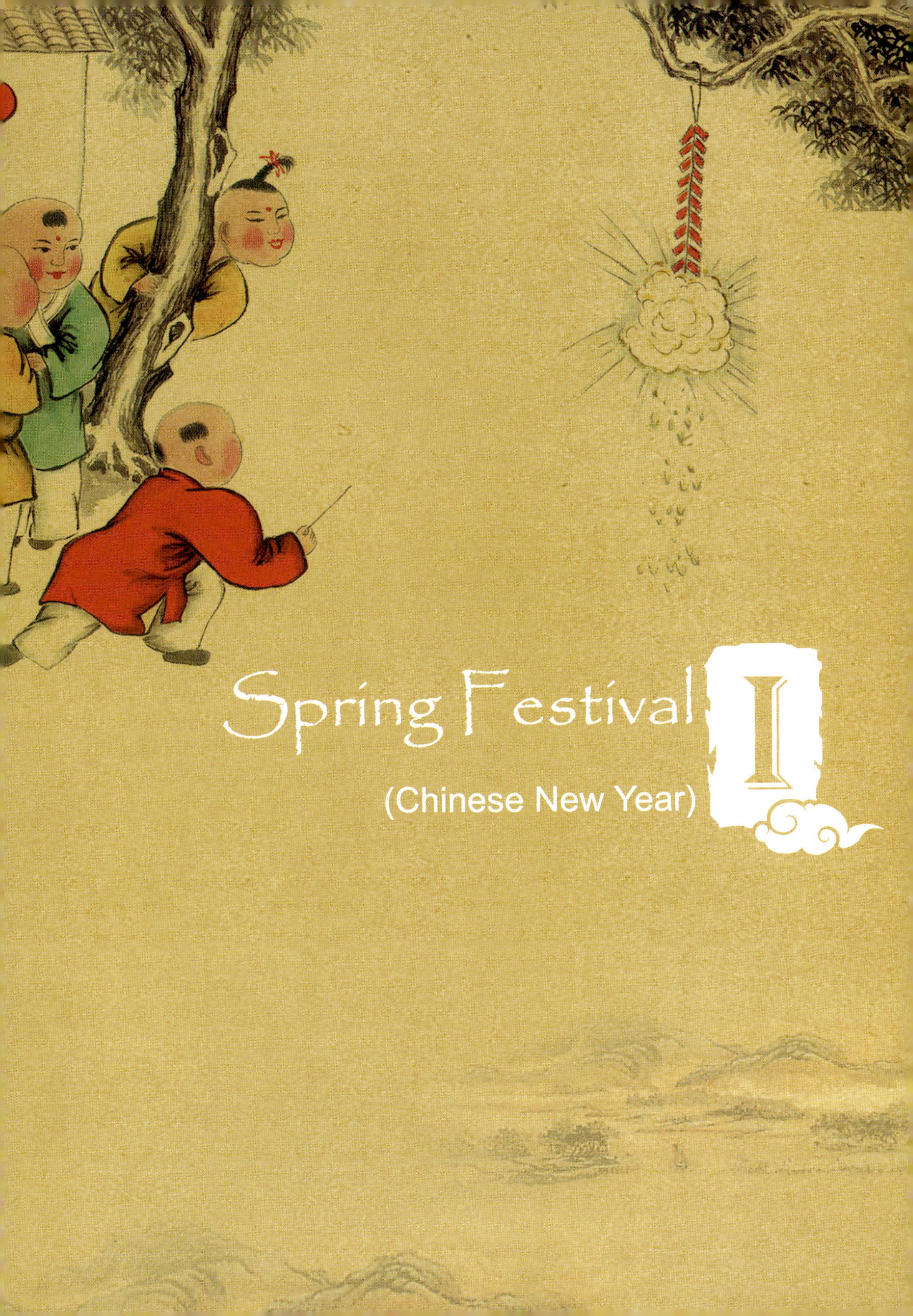

Spring Festival I
(Chinese New Year)

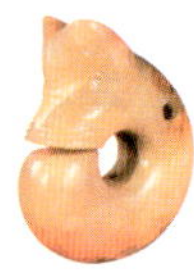

The Origin of "*Nian*" or the "Year"

The Spring Festival, also known as the Chinese New Year, is the major holiday in China.

The reason the ancients set the beginning of the year during the coldest days of the year is that this period falls right between the winter slack season and the season for spring planting, an opportunity for farmers to celebrate the harvest and to welcome

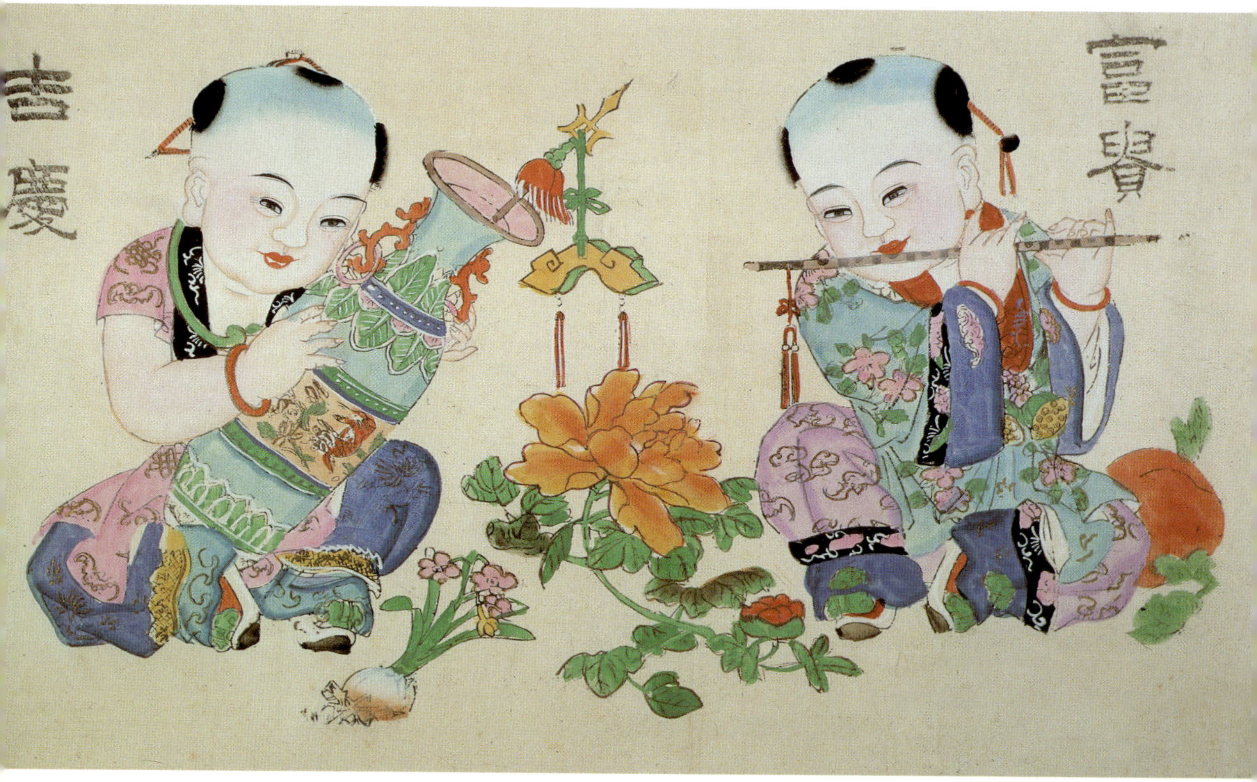

A New Year picture

the next farming season. Over time, it became a festival.

Chinese generally refer to the celebration of the Spring Festival as "*guo nian.*" The following was a story telling how this came about. A legendary vicious beast called *Nian* lived in the deep sea who would emerge from the waters at the turn of the year to destroy crops and harm people and cattle. One day, when it went to a village, *Nian* was scared away by a piece of red clothing hanging by the entrance of a house. It tried elsewhere, was scared off by lights and ran away. People came to the conclusion that this *Nian* must be afraid of loud noise, the color red and fire. At the turn of every year from then on, people would post red paper couplets at their doors, set off fire crackers, hang red lanterns, burn firewood and chop meat and vegetables as a way to expel this devilish beast.

"The Sound of Bamboo Cracking Sends off Another Year"

In his poem "The New Year Day," Wang Anshi (1021-1086), a prime minister of the Song Dynasty (960-1279), vividly describes the festival atmosphere of the New Year celebration: "The sound of bamboo cracking sends off another year, a spring breeze brings warmth and good wine drives away the evil spirits. Thousands of households celebrate this day, and new couplets take the place of old."

Originally, bamboo, not firecrackers, was burnt as a way to celebrate the New Year.   When bamboo burns, it expands and cracks, making a loud crackle. Firecrackers were a later invention,

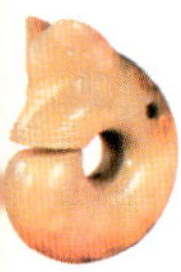

using gunpowder packed into bamboo stems at first, and it was not until much later that bamboo was replaced by tightly rolled paper tubes. By the end of the Qing Dynasty in the early 20th century, firecracker workshops could be found in every part of China.

"The noise of firecrackers, like huge waves and deafening thunder from every corner, went on throughout the night." Such was the scene on New Year's Eve in the Qing Dynasty as described in an old book. Firecrackers enhance the festive atmosphere of Chinese New Year and bring endless pleasure, especially to children.

"New Couplets Take the Place of Old"

At Chinese New Year, pictures of door-gods are posted, New Year couplets pasted and peach wood charms are hung on the door during the festival to ward off evil spirits.

The door-gods represent two Tang dynasty generals—Qin Qiong and Yuchi Gong. The legend goes that Li Shimin (599-649), the founding Emperor Taizong of the Tang Dynasty, became ill and had a nightmare in which he heard the howling and screaming of ghosts. The next day he recounted his bad dream to his subordinates, and Qin Qiong and Yuchi Gong, armed to the hilt, stood guard by his door through the night. That night, he had no nightmare. For all that he wanted peace, the emperor did not want the two generals to guard his door at all times and so he had artists paint pictures of the two—later known as door-gods—and hung them above the entrance to his palace. Later, the

▶ The tradition of setting off firecrackers to bring in the New Year has been kept to this day.

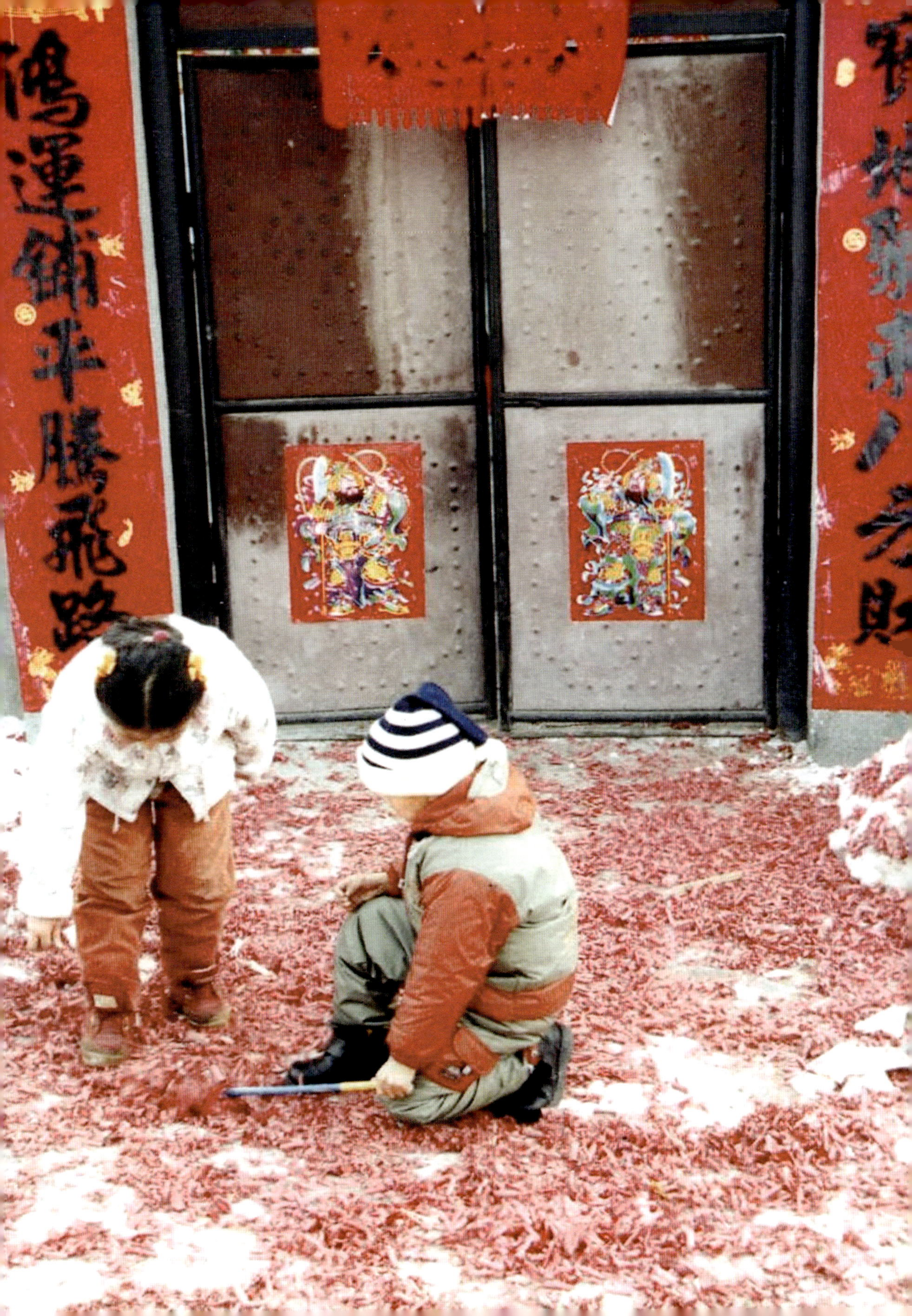

鴻運鋪平勝飛路
寶地發財

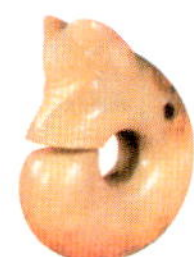

common people took up the idea and started posting pictures of door-gods during the Chinese New Year in order to ward off evil spirits.

Another traditional custom is the posting of New Year pictures, with themes ranging from good harvest and good luck to chubby baby and flowers and feathers. Places famous for their New Year pictures include Yangliuqing in Tianjin, Weifang in

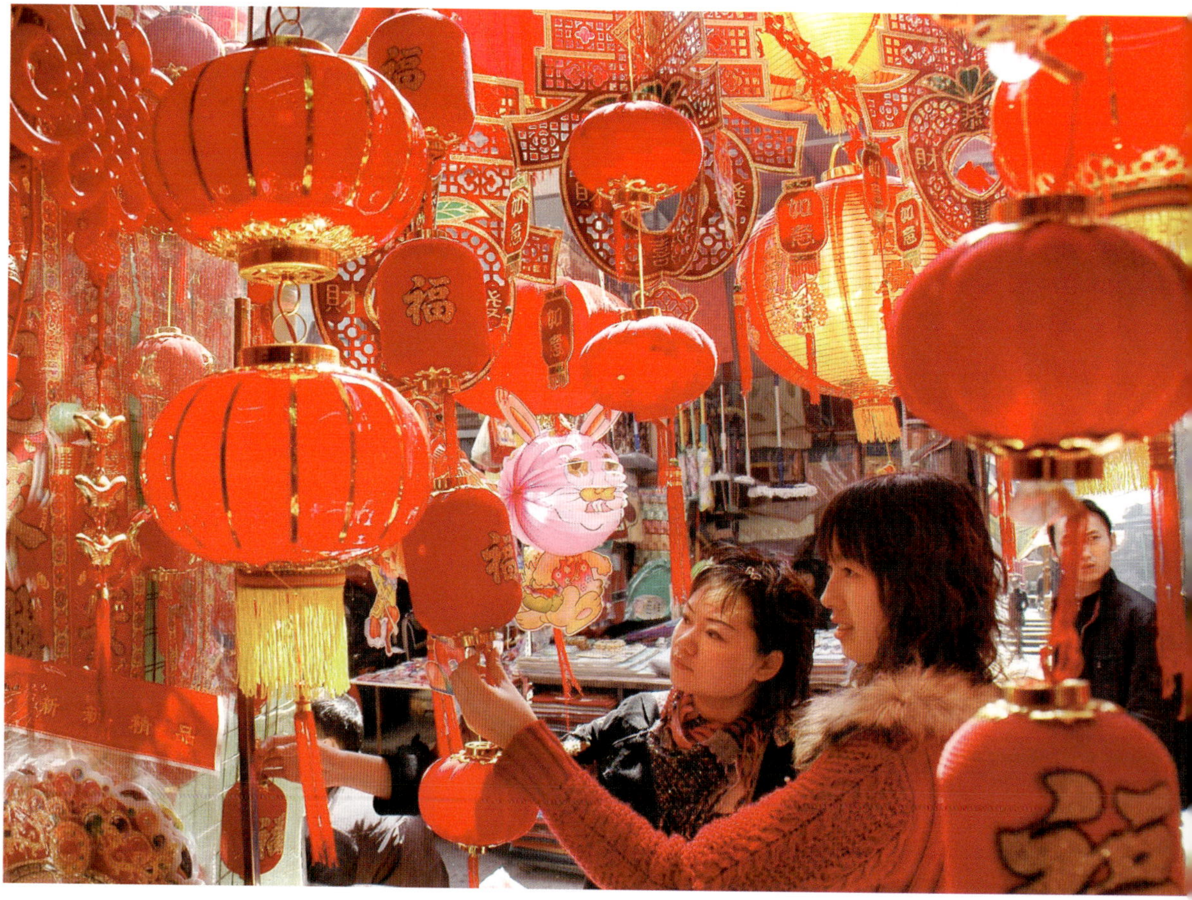

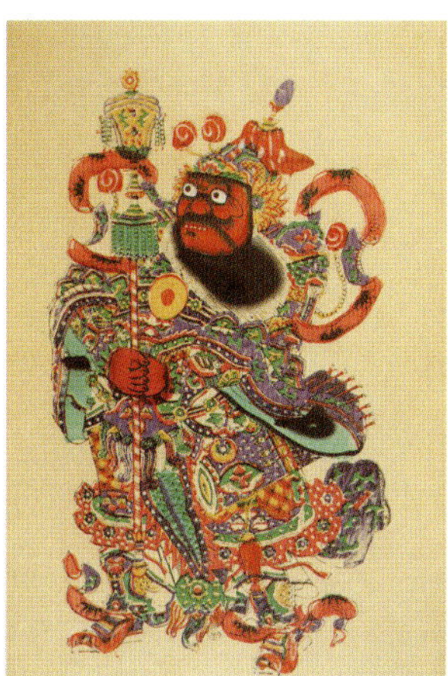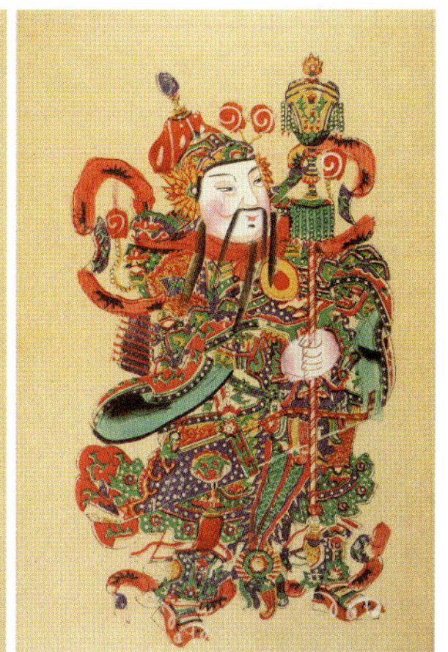

1. A joyous festive atmosphere in the streets during the Spring Festival
2. Picture of the Door-god

Shandong, Taohuawu in Suzhou, Mianzhu in Sichuan, Wuqiang in Hebei and Foshan in Guangdong.

Pasted on gateposts or door panels, New Year couplets are red scroll papers bearing auspicious phrases, for example—"Favorable weather and fertile land. Rich resources and outstanding talents"; "Peaceful times day in day out. Pleasant springtime year after year." New Year couplets originate from peach wood charms in the Spring and Autumn and Warring States periods more than 2,000 years ago. During the New Year, Taoist magic figures and incantations were written on two rectangular peach wood boards which were nailed onto door panels to ward off evil spirits. It was in Late Shu (934-965) of the Five Dynasties period that the custom started of writing couplets on peach wood boards. According to *History of Song*, *Family of Shu*, at New Year's Eve

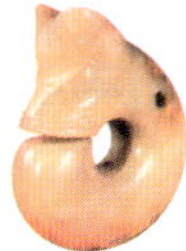

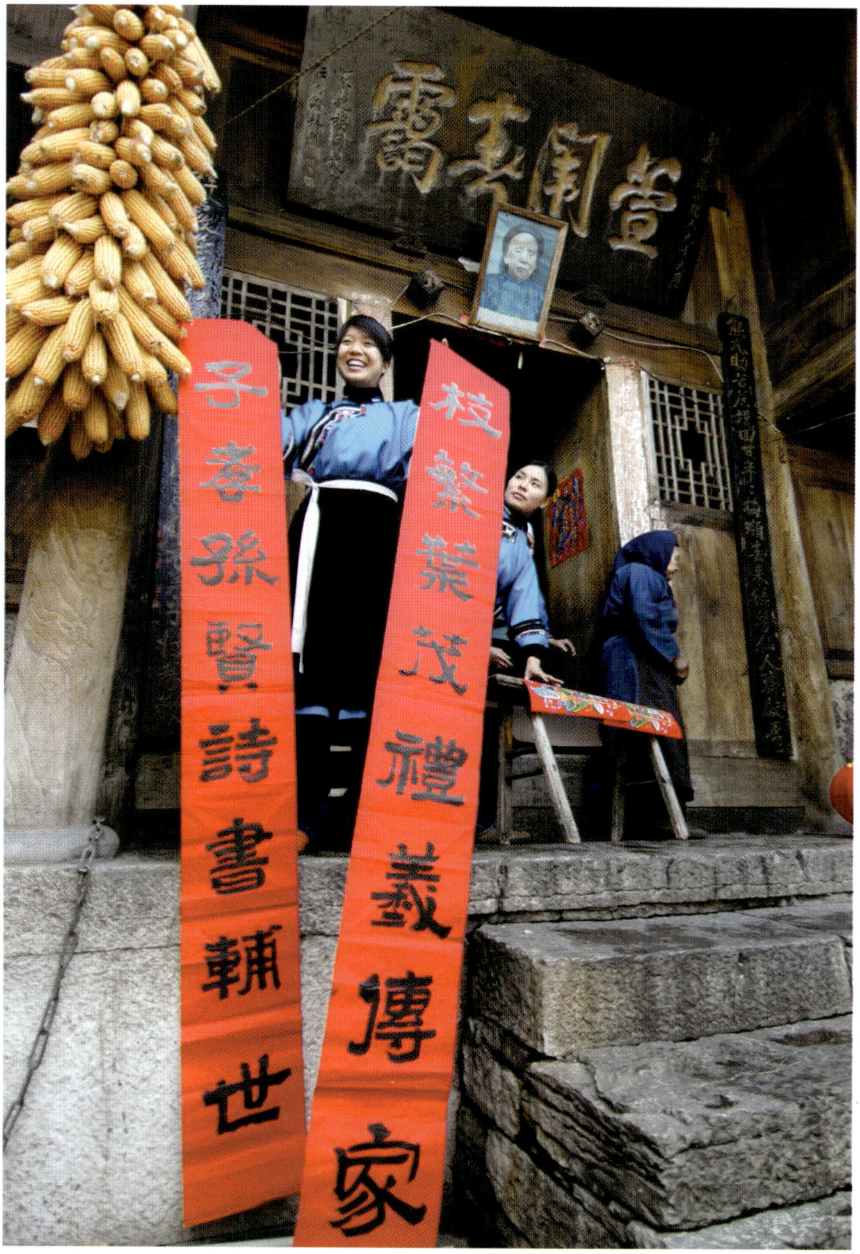

1. Putting up New Year couplets

2. New Year couplets decorating a household in a *hutong* (lane)

every year, Lord Meng Chang of the Late Shu would always ask scholars to write scriptures on peach wood boards, which he would hang on the doors of his bedroom. Not satisfied with the quality of their choice of words, he himself penned two lines: "The coming New Year will be blessed with the lingering happiness of the year just passed. The New Year heralds even more happiness." These are believed to be the first New Year couplets.

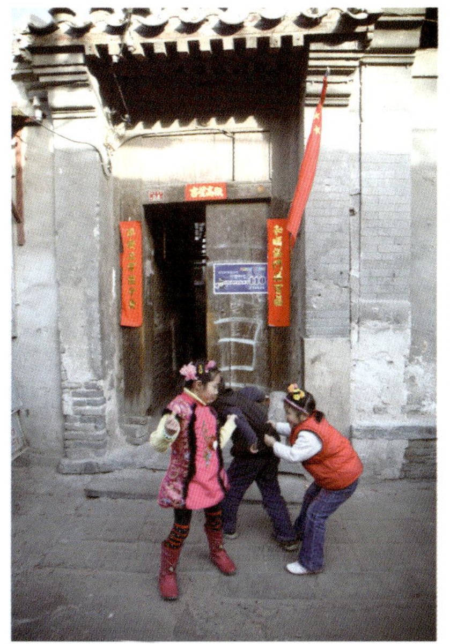

In the Song Dynasty, paper replaced wood for New Year couplets. Scholars and literati of the Imperial Academy liked to write and hang scrolls at the doors of the imperial palace. By the Ming dynasty (1368-1644), under the enthusiastic promotion of Emperor Tai Zu, pasting New Year couplets became even more popular.

Food Served at Chinese New Year

Spring Festival food is, of course, always more elaborate than at other times of the year. According to *Records of Festivities at the New Year in the Imperial Capital*, a book about old Beijing customs, food served during this time was almost exclusively

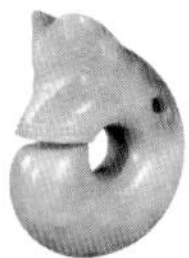

based on game and seafood delicacies, far beyond the pockets of ordinary people. In northern China, dumplings are the most popular food during the Spring Festival. Dumplings are served on the 30th day of the 12th lunar month and on the first day of the first lunar month. People like dumplings because of their convenience and taste. Dumplings are made into the shape of gold ingots to represent good fortune. Candies, coins, peanuts, dates and chestnuts are also put at random inside some of the dumplings: the lucky person who eats the candy dumpling will have a happy life in the year to come; whoever eats the coin dumpling will have enough money to spend; peanuts, also known as longevity nuts, symbolize long life; dates and chestnuts are signs of soon having a son.

In southern China, people wash enough rice to last the family several days—a "guarantee" of having surplus food every year. In addition to dishes of chicken, duck, fish and meat, there are also different kinds of dim sum snacks. Sticky cake made of glutinous rice flour—the stickier the better—is something that must be served around the New Year. In Chinese, the words for "sticky cake" sound the same as "ascending every year," indicating success. In Guangzhou, all kinds of steamed and deep fried dim sum made of glutinous rice, taro, shrimp and turnip are also served at this time of year. In Huai'an, in Jiangsu Province, lotus seed tea and dates, together with candies, watermelon seeds, dates and sticky cake are served as starters while lucky phrases such as "may your life be sweet," "may your life get better," and "may you have a son soon" are said to wish everyone good luck. In Shaoxing in Zhejiang Province, at tea time on the first day of

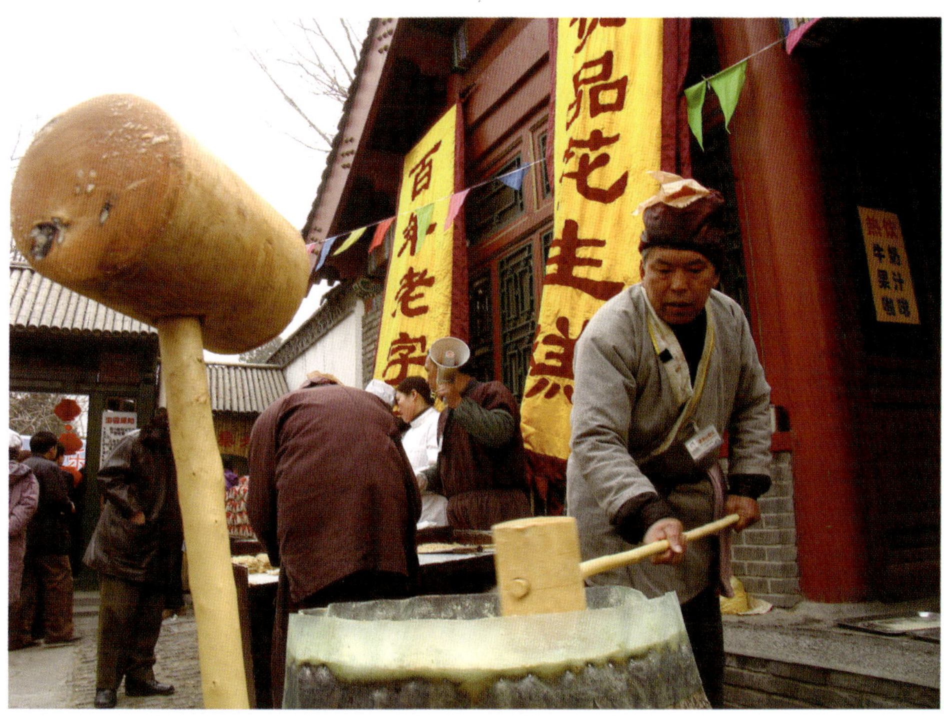

Making sticky-rice cake

the year, olive and kumquat are added to the tea. For breakfast, balls of pounded sticky rice, sweet and round, are served to suggest family reunion. For older people, vegetarian food is always preferred.

Elaborate Dinner on New Year's Eve

On the eve of the Chinese New Year, all members of the family will come together over a dinner. In northern China, these dinners consist mainly of dumplings, but in the south things are more elaborate. In cities such as Hangzhou, Suzhou and

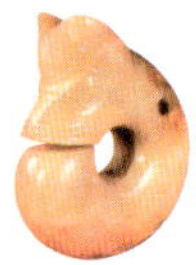

Shanghai, the dinner must also include dumplings but egg is used rather than wheat flour to make the outside wrap, and pork is used for the fillings. Then the egg dumplings are put on top of spinach and thin bean flour vermicelli in a clay pot and boiled. The dumplings, which look like bags of gold sitting on top of green and white, are a feast for both eye and stomach alike. Another essential dish is pork and shredded bamboo shoot stir-fry to

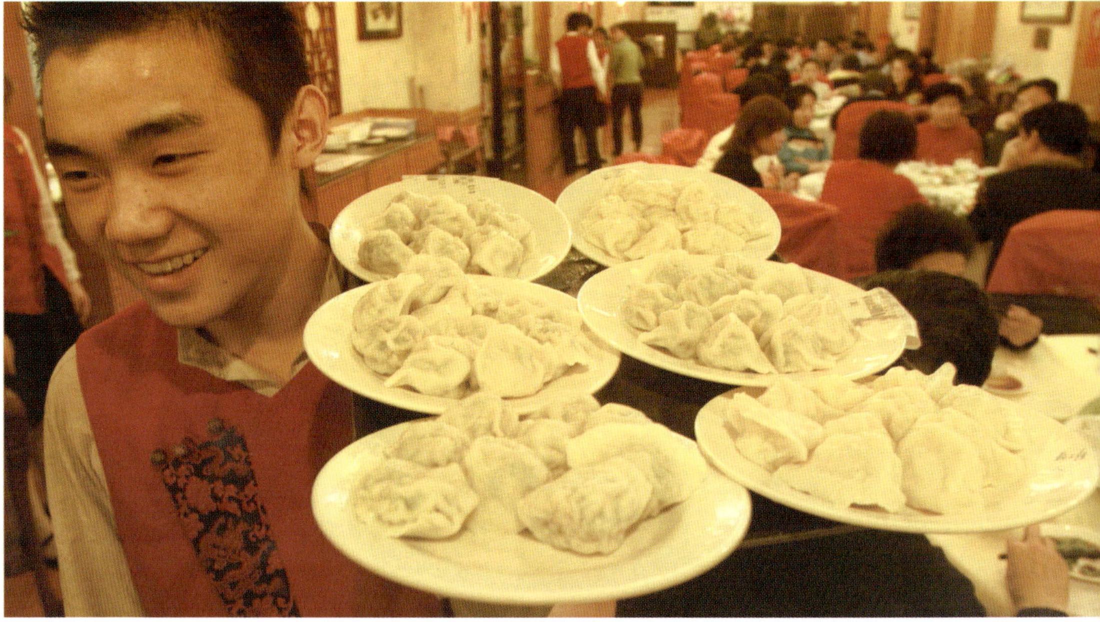

Eating dumplings to celebrate Chinese New Year

suggest that all will be well in the coming year. A bowl of meatballs is served to mean family reunion. There is also a bowl of sliced pork head and a bowl of eggs boiled in soy sauce. Everyone must have an egg so that the family will continue for generations to come. A whole fish, complete with head and tail, must also be served. The head and tail should not be consumed so everything will have a good beginning and end. At the dinner, everyone— young and old—must take a sip of rice wine, imparting a warm glow in all, as if spring has already come.

In Taiwan, all members of the family sit around the table to eat hot pot. Appetizers and wine are served and vegetables, which are not cut, must be eaten whole to wish the elders a

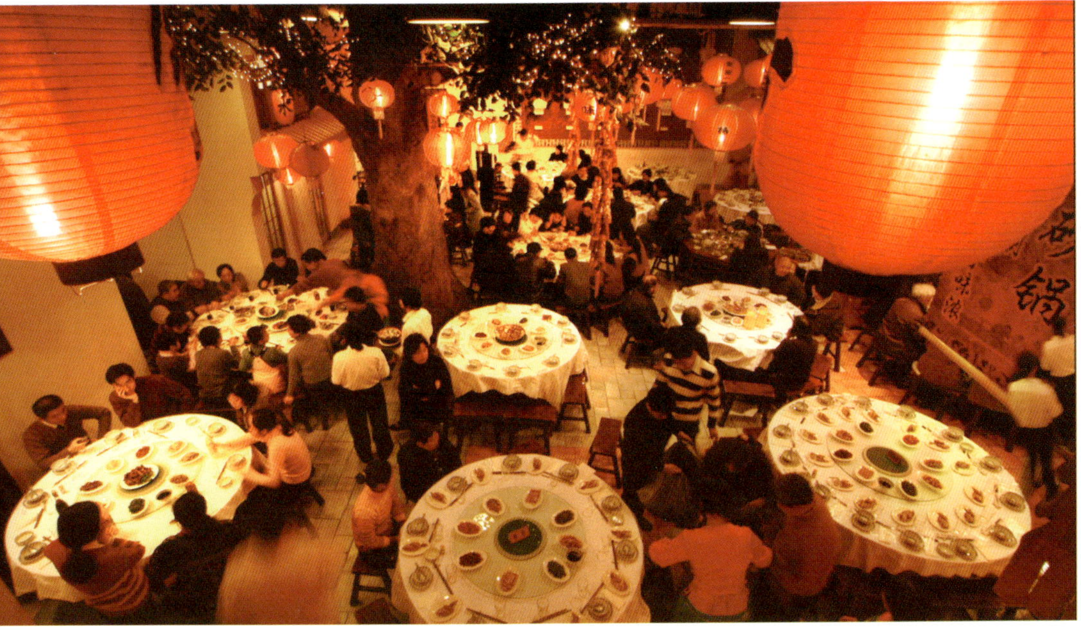

A family reunion dinner during the Spring Festival

long life. If a family member is unable to join the dinner, an empty chair with his or her clothes is reserved as a reminder of the absentee.

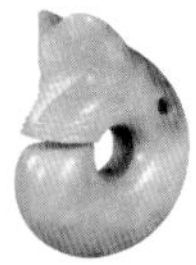

Staying Awake on New Year's Eve

After the New Year's Eve dinner, no one is supposed to go to bed. Kids certainly would not miss this rare and happy opportunity. Men sit and chat while the wives busy themselves cooking for the New Year. Everyone stays awake to make sure that the old year passes and the new year comes in peacefully.

On this special night, oil lamps are lit inside and outside the house and next to the stove so that the lights scare off all unlucky things. In Hangzhou, there is an old custom of climbing Wu, or City God, Hill. From the top, the city looks spectacular with lights from every household and fireworks of every form and color. Ancestors are worshipped with five-colored paper money, fruit and nuts.

A thorough cleaning must be carried out to make the home look clean and to boost the spirits. In the past, when the poor were unable to repay a debt, they had to hide from the lender, who might come to their house to demand payment, which would spoil the otherwise joyous New Year occasion. On the New Year's Eve in Taiwan people used to play a show called "Dodging Debt" in front of temples, where debtors would come to watch. If a lender dared go up to the stage and ask the debtor for payment, the audience would boo the lender, rather than one who owed money.

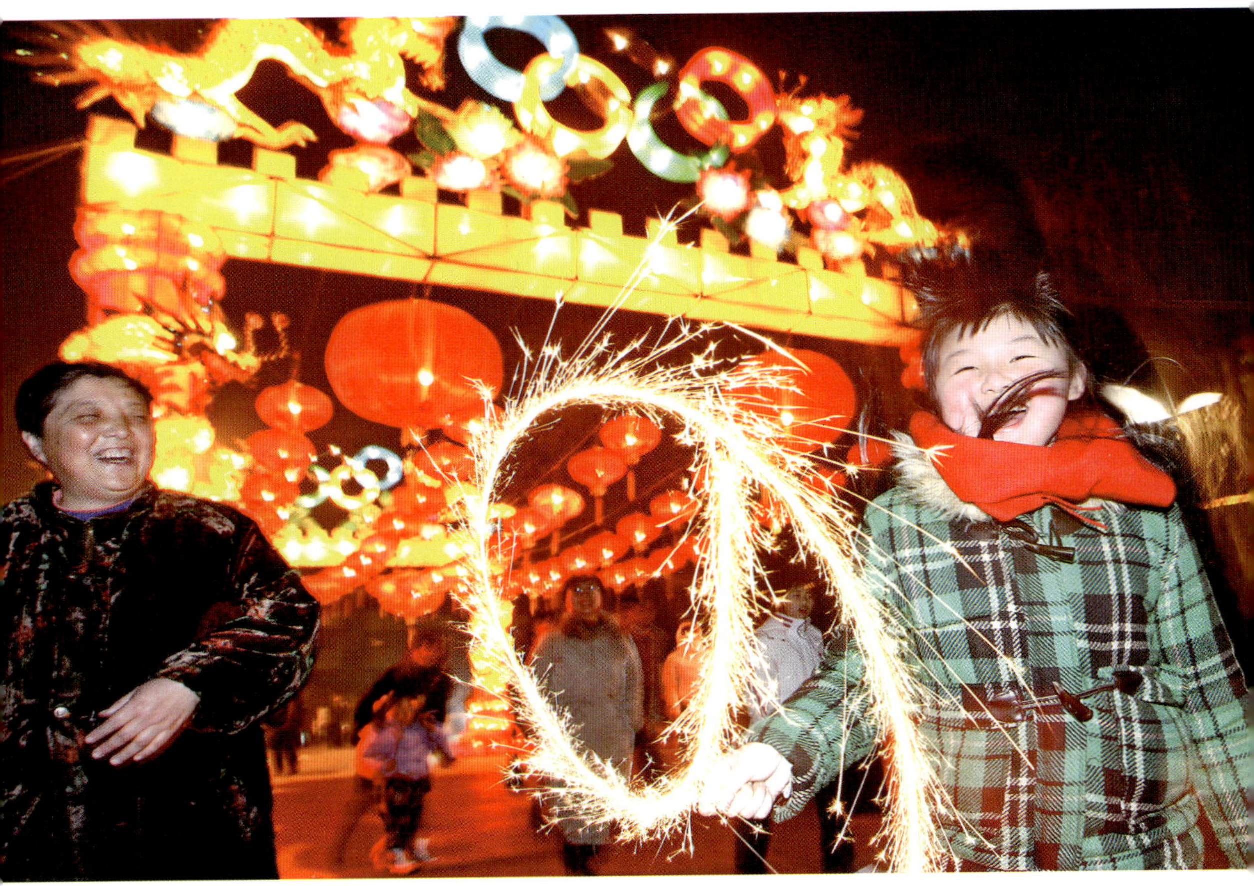

A festival scene of fireworks

New Year's Activities

The New Year arrives at midnight. In the old times, the first thing people did on this first morning of the New Year was to light firecrackers and burn incense as a way of welcoming the gods and worshipping their ancestors. On New Year's Day itself, everyone—young and old, men and women—put on their new clothes and visit the homes of relatives to pay their New Year respects. On this occasion, people bow to each other,

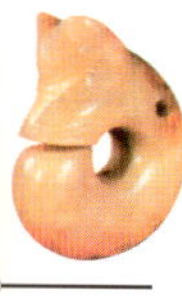

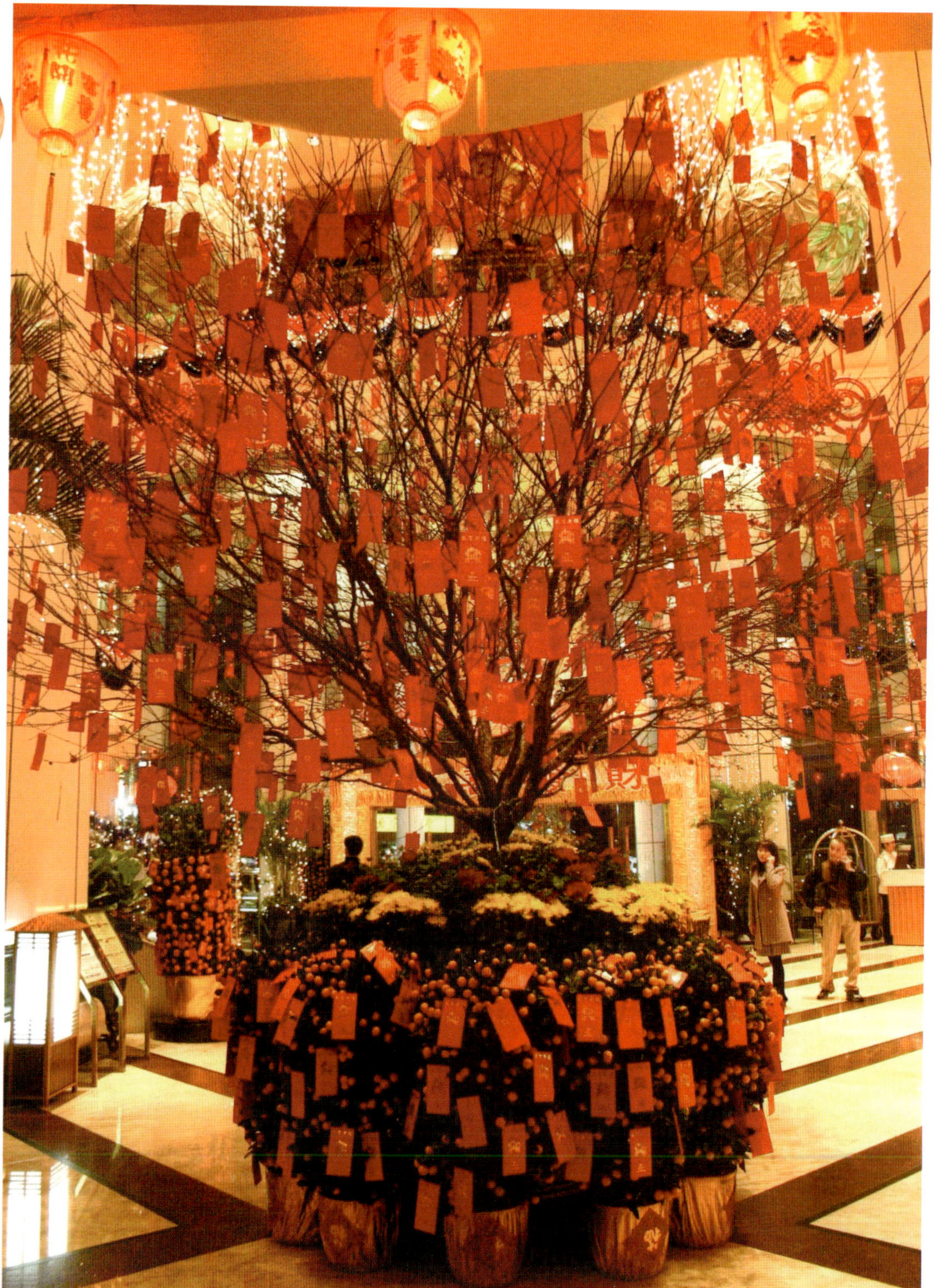

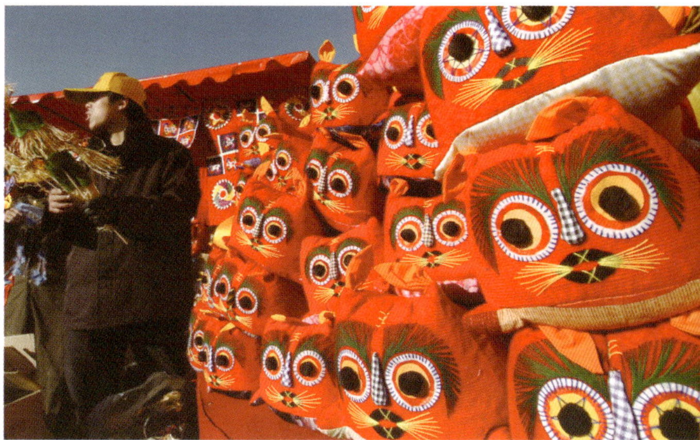

1. Nowadays, it is a common practice for shops to have a tree decorated with red envelopes, as a symbol of good fortune and wealth.
2. Children wear red "tiger-head" shoes during the Spring Festival to keep away evil and pray for blessings.

kowtow, uttering such greetings as "Wish you a prosperous year," "Kong Hay Fat Choi," "May you get your desire in all things," and "May you have a happy and long life." Children utter New Year greetings to their elders, receiving in return red envelopes containing New Year gift money. Pockets full of gift money, the kids would buy firecrackers and their favorite goodies, and play to their heart's content. On this day, no one works; it's all just sitting around, chatting, eating well and playing as much as one pleases.

People start visiting their relatives and friends after breakfast on the second day, bringing along gifts such as glutinous rice cake, oranges and candies. When they arrive, the host gives them tea or a cigarette and they chat for a while before leaving for the next family. Some go to temples where they get together and picnic.

The third day of the New Year is known as the "day of sending poverty away." On this day, people would not go visiting.

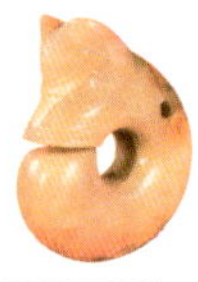

Instead, they would sweep away dirt and broken bones, dump them into fields and burning them. While doing so, they have to burn incense and pray, thus banishing poverty and ill luck and inviting fortune and good luck.

The fourth day is also the happiest time for wives. On this day, the wives—dressed in their best and taking their children and gifts with them—return to the home of their parents.

There is a belief that all the gods in heaven come down to earth to inspect on the fifth day. People normally put fruit and food in front of the statues of these gods and worship them in the hope that they will bring good fortune to their house.

Between the first and the fifteenth day of the New Year, there are all kinds of activities.

Drumming Contests and Lion Dances

Drumming contests and lion dances are very popular in villages of southern China, and from the first to the fifteenth day of the New Year festivities the sound of drumbeats can be heard. Each village has a drum team, comprising a drum, bronze cymbals and several bronze gongs, and they compete with drum teams from other villages. The cymbals clash and the gongs resound following the drumbeats, coming to a climax when every team beats as hard as possible to produce the loudest sound. The beating of the drum sounds like strong wind and ocean waves and ten thousand horses running in the fields, making the otherwise quiet village full of life.

▶ A dragon dance

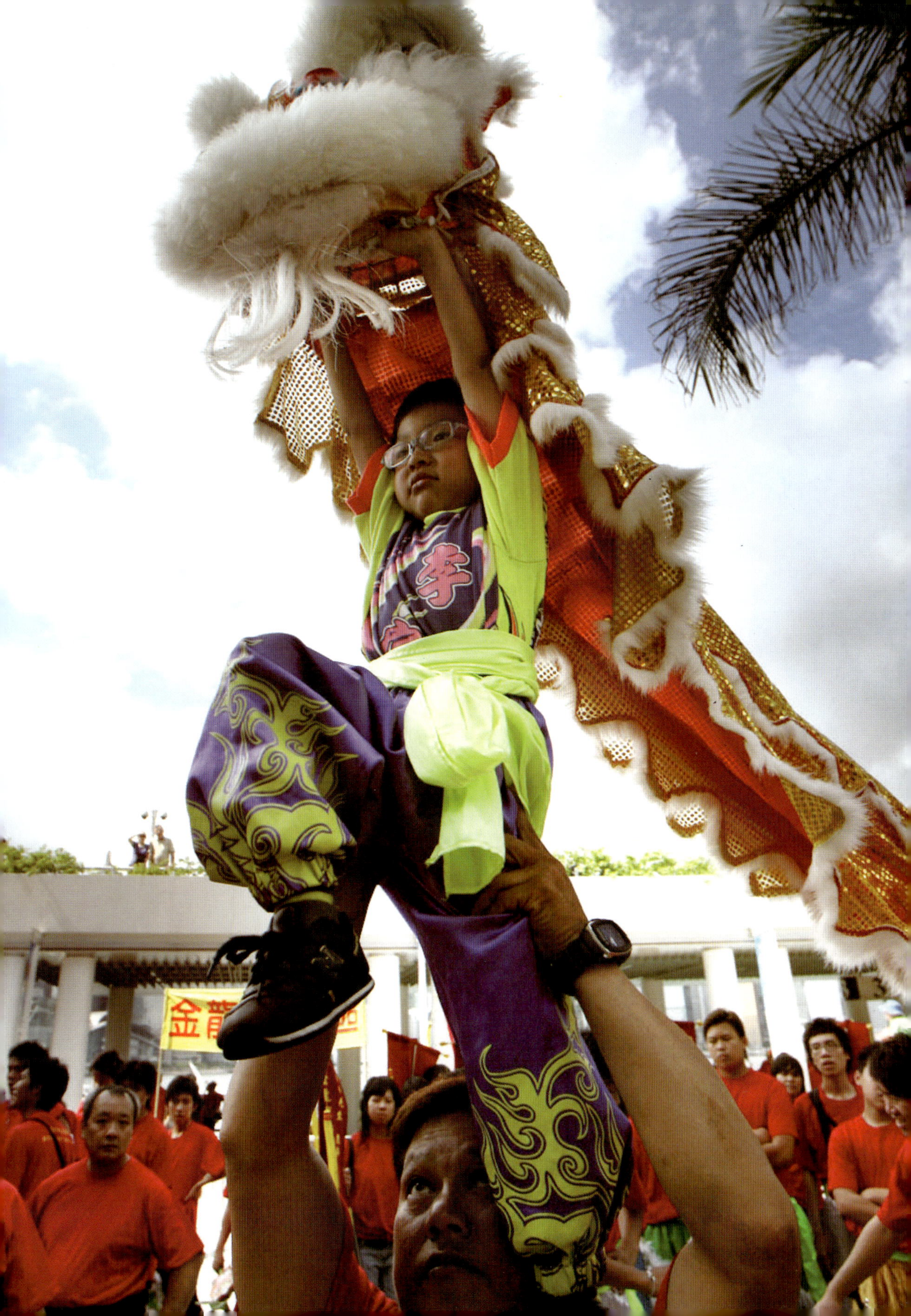

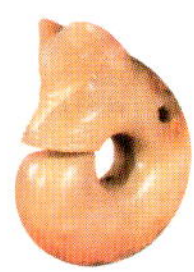

From the fourth to the fifteenth day of the festival, lion dancers wind through the villages. A lion-dance team consists of seven to a dozen people; all are dressed alike, wielding spears and clubs, to resemble warriors. The lion's head is made of paper and there are "cat-head, "rooster-head" and "fighting bull" lions named according to the form of the head. These paper heads are brightly painted and draped with fabrics as colorful as the body of the lion. One dancer holds the head and the others bend over, one holding the tail. To the beating of drums and gongs, and with a guide directing the lion at the front, the dancers perform all kinds of movements—"lion playing with silk ball," "warrior teasing the lion," "frolicking lions" and "lion with cubs," for example.

Other folk entertainment activities include stilt-walking, dragon lantern dance, "land boat" dance and bamboo horses. Traditional operas such as "Monkey King Fighting with the White-bone Demon Three Times" and "Legend of the White Snake" are also performed.

Beijing's Changdian and Guangzhou's Flower Fair

China's temple and street fairs go back into history. Full of ethnic and local color, such New Year fairs help bring city and country folks into contact and invigorate the market.

The Changdian street fair in Beijing was already famous back in the Qing Dynasty (1644-1911). Held at Liulichang, between the first and fifteenth day of the festival, the fair attracted people from far and wide. Stalls selling all kinds of things—food, daily goods, toys, calligraphy, paintings and antiques—lined both sides of the street. Platforms were also set up for Peking Opera and acrobatic shows. People from every walk of life and economic background could revel in the joys of the fair. It was heaven for children too; for a modest sum they could get toffee-coated haws on a stick, colorful kites of every shape and color or fancy paper pinwheels. *Record of Changdian*, a book written in the Qing Dynasty, states: "Usually Changdian is empty, with few people visiting. But during the first lunar month, ladies from all over the city arrive on foot or by vehicle, crowding the place."

Guangzhou's Flower Fair is also a New Year street fair

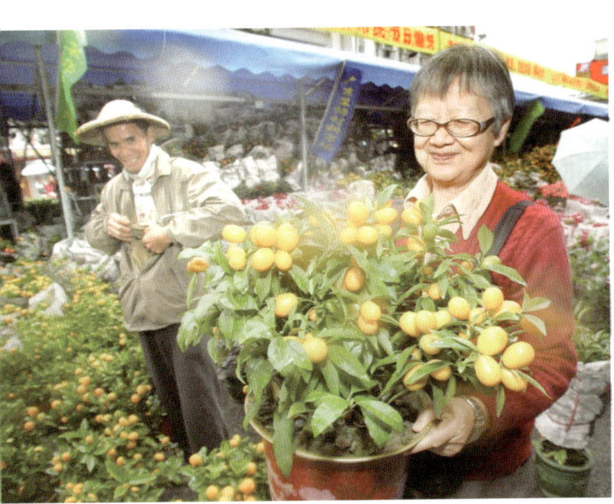

Guangzhou's Flower Fair

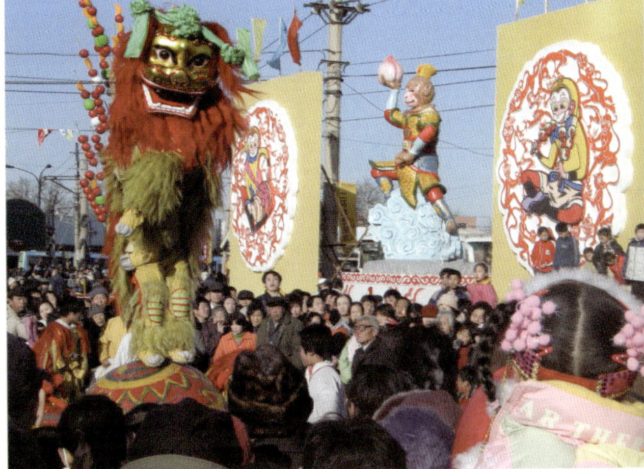

Changdian street fair in Beijing

that attracts people from all over. It starts three days before Chinese New Year's Day and ends at 2:30 in the morning of New Year's Day.

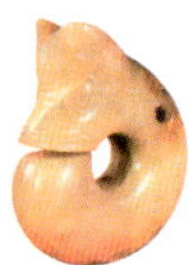

Because of its southern location, Guangzhou has a mild climate throughout the year. During the time of Chinese New Year, flowers raised in the Guangzhou suburbs and the neighboring nine counties along the Pearl River flood the streets and lanes, covering the city with waves of gorgeous peach blossom, elegant chrysanthemum, graceful narcissus, and kumquat, the symbol of good luck....At the flower fair, people also get to see the famous palace lanterns made in Foshan, while enjoying the light and smooth music of Guangdong Province.

Stilt-walking

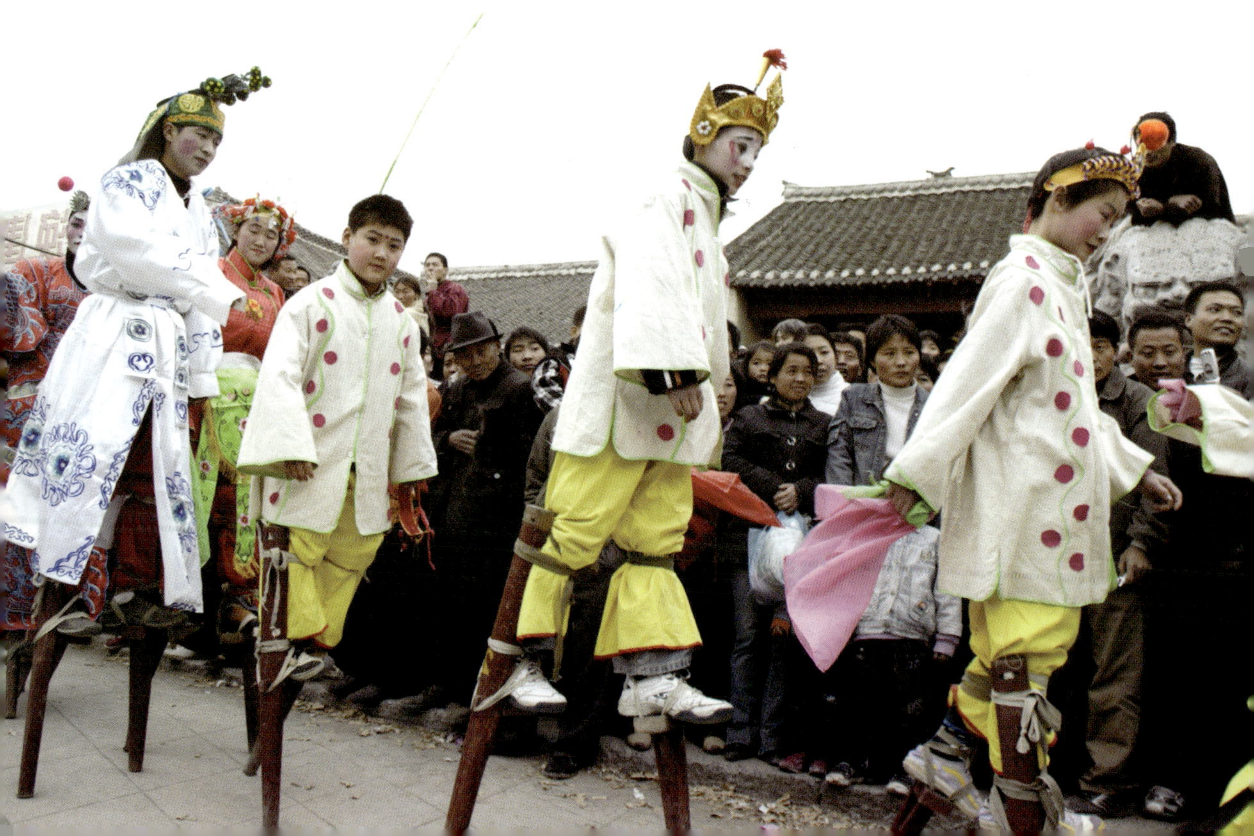

Chinese New Year in the Ming and Qing Palaces

In the Ming and Qing dynasties the imperial throne attached great importance to Chinese New Year and ceremonies were even more elaborate.

On Chinese New Year's Day, the ceremony of paying respect to the emperor was enacted. The day before the ceremony, a throne was set up in the Hall of Sacrifice to Heaven and, before daybreak on New Year's Day, the imperial guard of honor and carriages would line up flanking the path up to the Hall of Sacrifice to Heaven, while flags fluttered above the Gate of Sacrifice to Heaven. Flanking the way between the Hall of Sacrifice to Heaven and the Meridian Gate were the imperial guard. The drum was beaten thrice; the emperor appeared on his throne; civilian officials and military officers kowtowed. A delegate read out a congratulatory statement from a tablet, eulogizing the emperor's achievements, upon which the emperor responded by asking everyone present to join him in celebrating the festival. Then the delegate raised the tablet in both hands, and the officials bowed, hands folded, shouting "Long Live the Emperor" three times. The imperial guards did the same. When the music and firecrackers started, the emperor rose, returning to his chamber, followed by the officials. After the ceremony, a grand banquet was held.

In the Qing Dynasty, a New Year's Eve banquet was held at the Hall of Preserving Harmony. This was attended mainly by leaders of ethnic groups, envoys from foreign countries and other high-ranking officials. Ninety tables of food and wine were

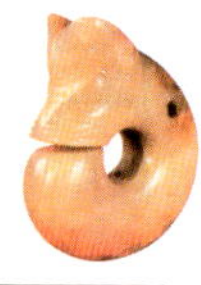

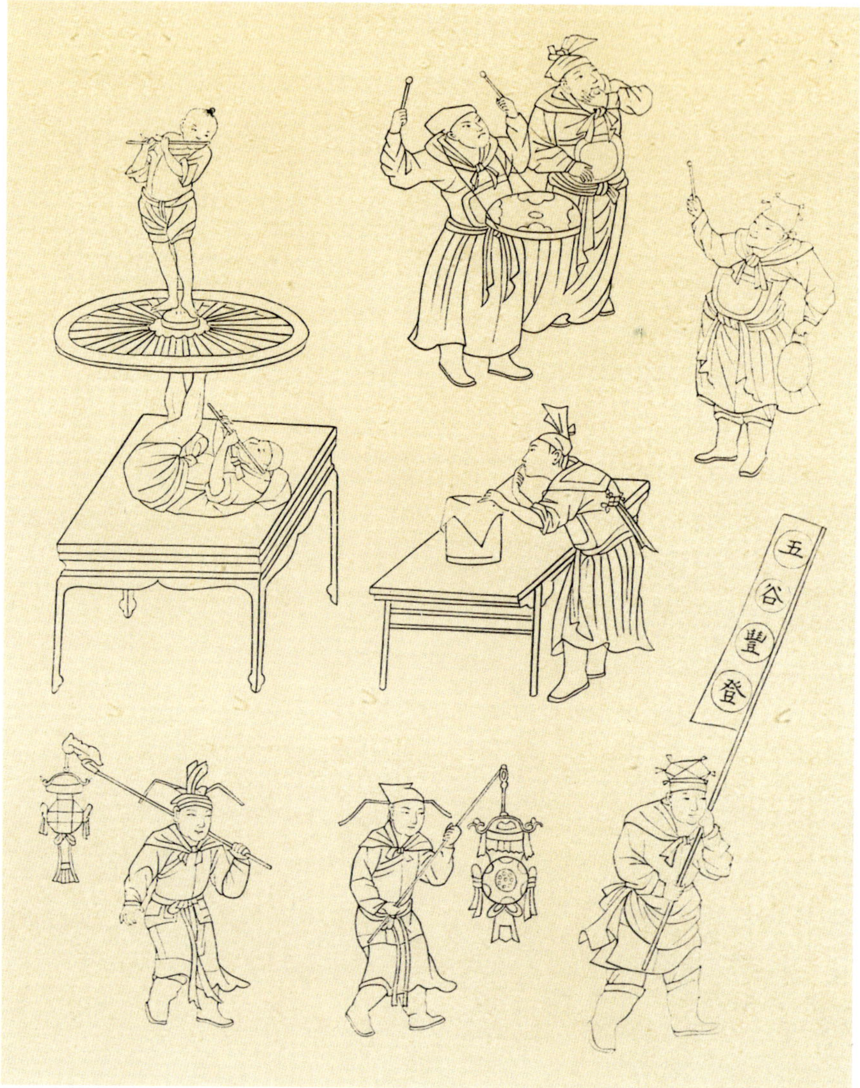

1 | 2

1. All types of performances at a temple fair

2. Today's temple fair

prepared on both sides of the hall. The floor was covered with coir rugs and felts. The guests—two per table—all sat cross-legged on the floor.

When the emperor appeared at his seat, all would kowtow to him before sitting themselves; likewise, no one drank before the emperor had done so. There would be a brief burst of music and when it stopped the eating began. At this point, Mongolian, Tibetan and Muslim music was played. Princes, dukes and imperial bodyguards, about a dozen altogether, would start to dance the "happy dance" in pairs. One team of guards would sing

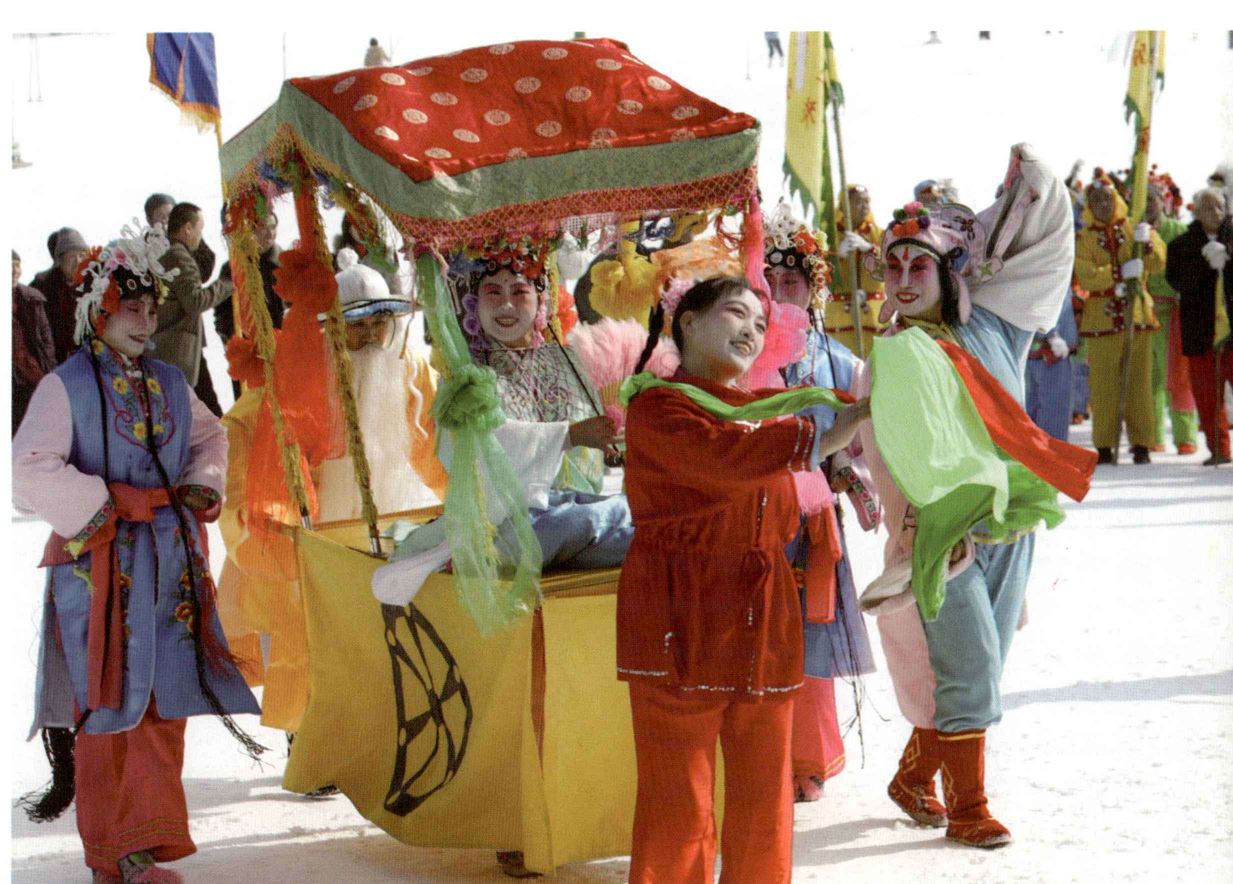

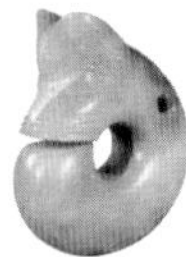

in Manchurian as musical accompaniment to the dance while another team would produce sounds by scraping chopsticks on wicker scoop. After these performances, performances would start outside the hall, including battle dances, high-stilt walking, Korean tumbling, and acrobatics. The last dance was the lion dance, at the end of which the emperor would rise from his seat, his subordinates would kowtow to him and then stand up.

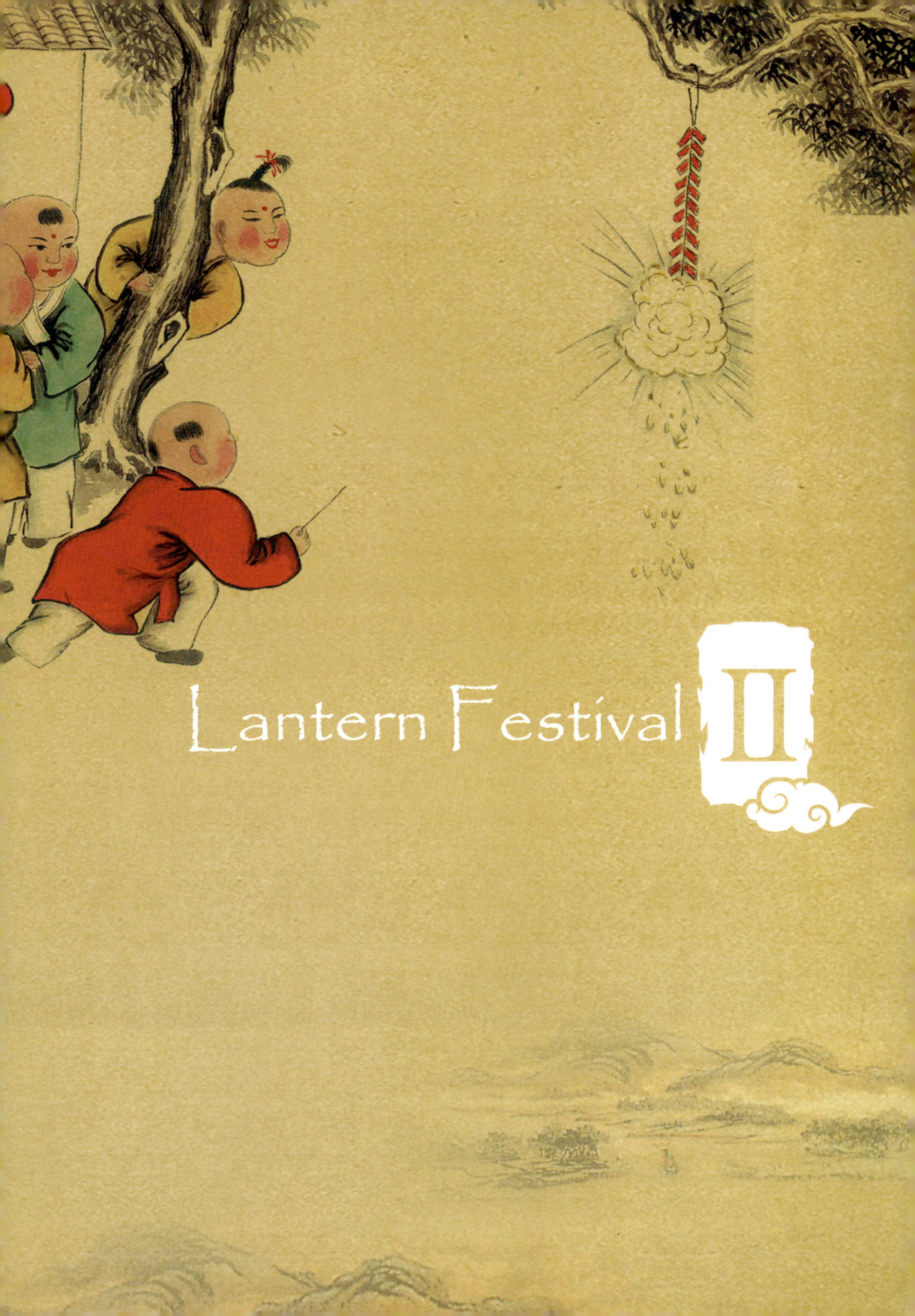
Lantern Festival II

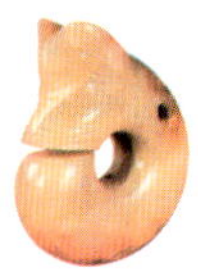

Origin of the Lantern Festival

Falling on the fifteenth day of the first lunar month, the Lantern Festival falls on the first full-moon night after Chinese New Year when families would get together to celebrate. Lanterns of every form and shape would be lit on this night, which is how the festival got its name.

The practice of viewing lanterns and admiring the moon can be traced back as far as the Warring States period in the third century B.C, when it was a ceremony to worship the god of the sun. After the death of the Han Emperor Liu Ying (221-194 B.C.), his mother, Empress Lü, usurped the throne. After her death, ministers who had remained loyal to the Han emperor purged all the Lü faction on the fifteen day of the first lunar month, installing Liu Heng who, as the Han Emperor (202-157 B.C.), restored the country to prosperity. To celebrate this day, the emperor decided that it should become the Lantern Festival.

Lantern Viewing

According to *Record of East Capital*, a book about Kaifeng, the capital of the Northern Song Dynasty, "on the night of the fifteenth day of the first lunar month, visitors gather beneath the big tent of the imperial court to sing and to dance. The music can be heard for miles."

Lantern viewing had much to do with the night curfew enforced since the Zhou Dynasty more than 2,000 years ago. Such strictness was at odds with the festival atmosphere of Chinese New Year. According to *Shiji*, or *Records of the*

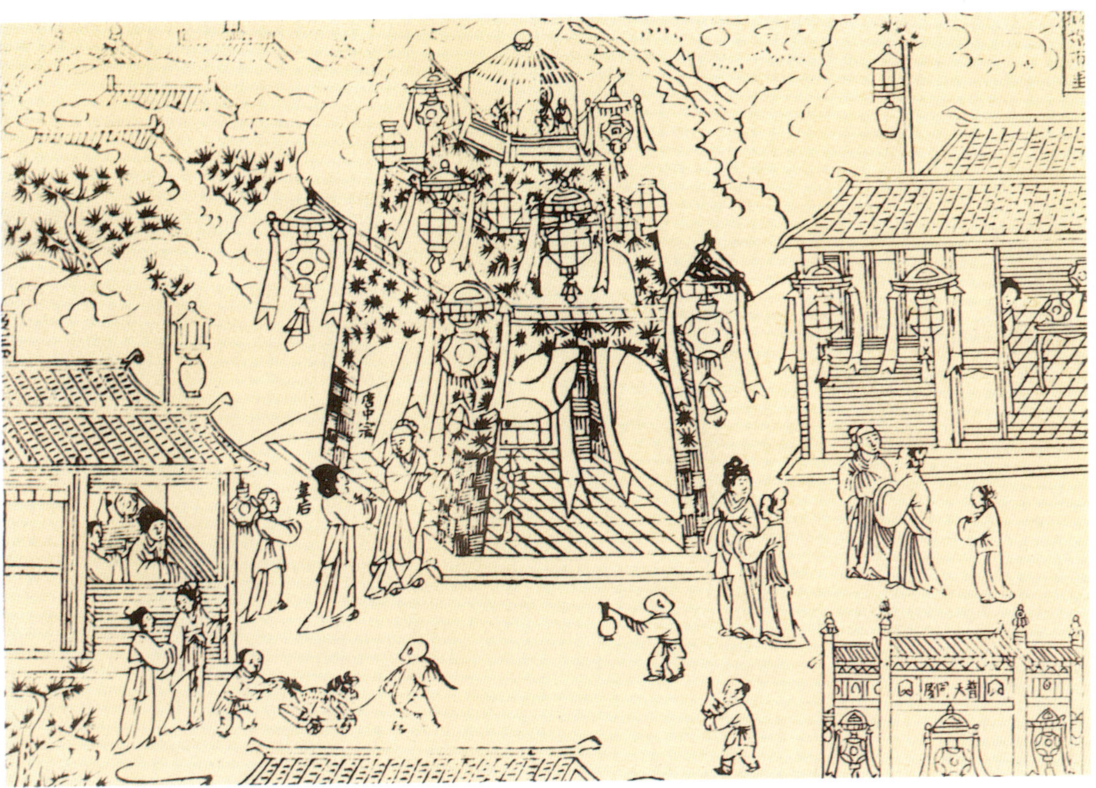

A lantern fair during the Lantern Festival in ancient China

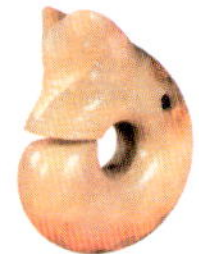

Historian, which was written in the first century BC, the ceremony of worshipping heaven on the fifteenth day of the first lunar month could be held throughout the night. This was the start of relaxing the strict rules and also the origin of viewing lanterns at night. Actually, lighting lanterns became very popular in the fifth and sixth centuries during the period of the Southern and Northern Dynasties.

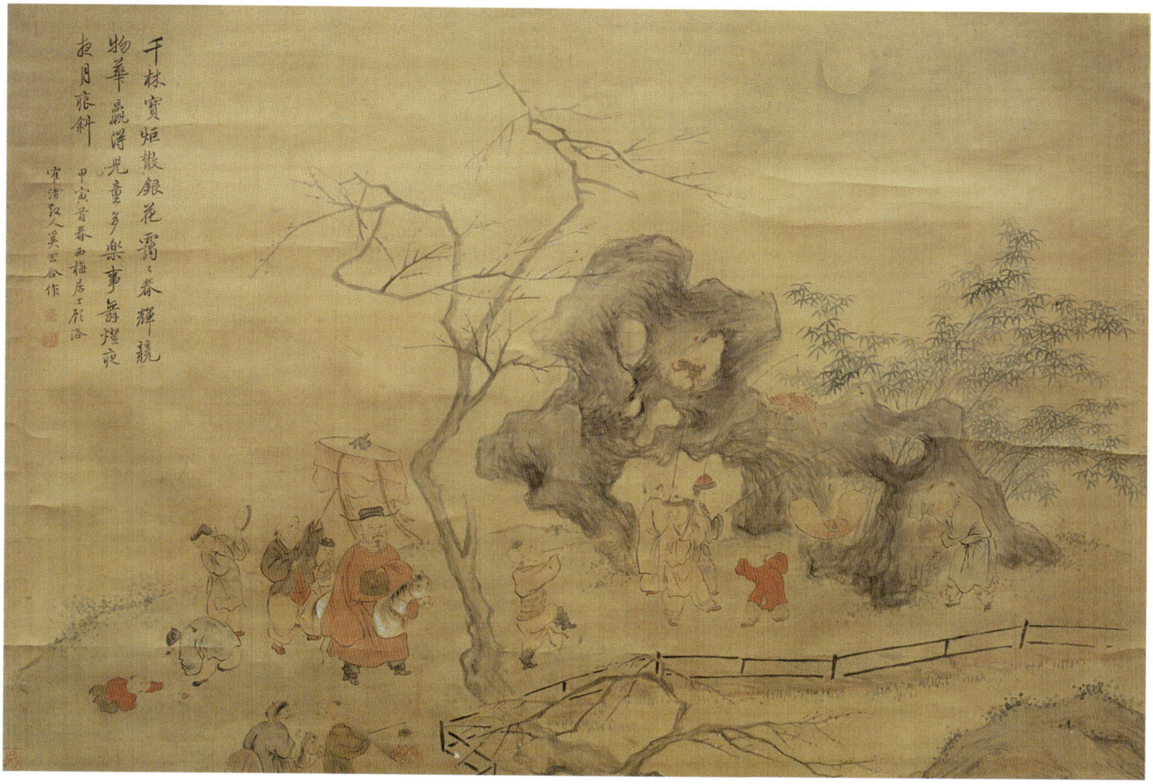

An ancient painting of people carrying lanterns to celebrate the Lantern Festival

In the Tang Dynasty (618-907), the Lantern Festival and the days preceding and following it were official holidays. On these nights, there was no curfew and people could enjoy themselves without constraint. Even the palace gate was open to the public. In the second year of the Tang Emperor Xuanzong (713 AD), the palace gate opened to the public on the night of

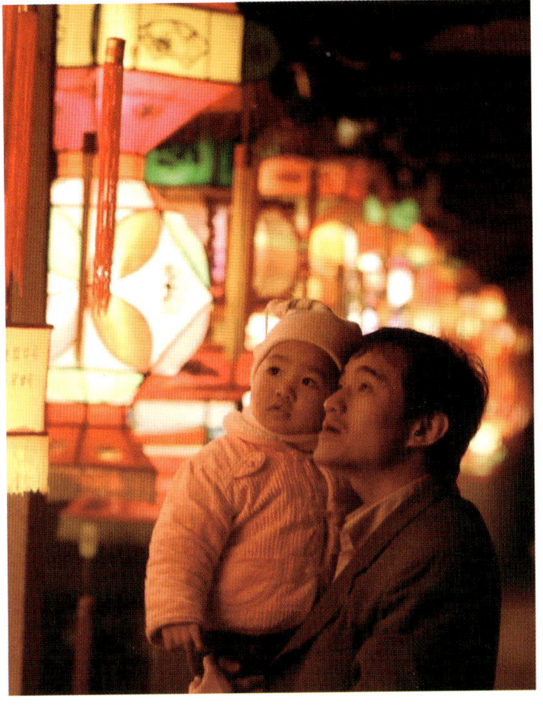

the Lantern Festival. Outside the palace, a "lantern wheel over twenty feet high was set up… 50,000 candles were lit, looking like a tree of flowers." "In addition, several thousand palace girls and about one thousand girls and young women from Chang'an city, the Tang capital, were ordered to sing below the lantern wheel for three days and nights." (See *Golden Record of Court and Commonalty*) From that time on, emperors of succeeding dynasties would view lanterns along with the common people on this festival. Tents and towers for displaying lanterns were built near the palace, temples, monasteries, and houses of the rich. During the Song Dynasty, the viewing period was extended from three nights to five, and a cup of free wine was bestowed on every viewer as an incentive to come out and see the lanterns.

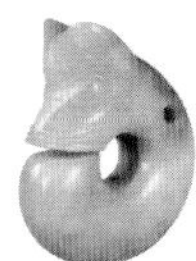

Today's Lantern Festival includes swings, dragon lantern dance, firecrackers, high stilts, "land boat" dancing under a bright full moon casting its light over thousands of colorful lanterns.

The Lantern Festival raised lantern making into an art form in its own right. The tale goes that over 2,000 years ago, in the Warring States Period, the renowned master carpenter Lu Ban started to make palace lanterns when he built palaces. The lanterns fall into various categories: famous figure lanterns tell legends of "Chang E Flying to the Moon," "Xishi Picking Lotus" and "Liu Hai Playing with a Toad;" flower lanterns feature lotus, grapes, melons, lotus root, peony, persimmons and oranges; animal lanterns depict deer, crane, dragon, horse, monkey, phoenix, goldfish, carp, frog and shrimp. The traditional revolving-horse lantern—one with a revolving circle of paper-cut horses or other figures—gets its name from the generals on horseback painted on the lantern. On the bottom of such lanterns is a wheel propelled by heat from a burning candle, which causes the paper lantern to revolve like a carousel. This type also depicts such well-known stories as "Monkey King Fighting the White Bone Demon Three Times," "Peacock Spreading its Tail," "Heavenly Girl Throwing Flowers from the Sky" and "Gold Fish Spitting Pearl." In China's Northeast, people use ice to make all manner of ice lanterns and sculptures. Materials such as bamboo, iron, wood, rattan, wheat stalks and animal horn can be used to make the lantern structure; paper, silk, even glass or plastic sheet can be used as the outside cover.

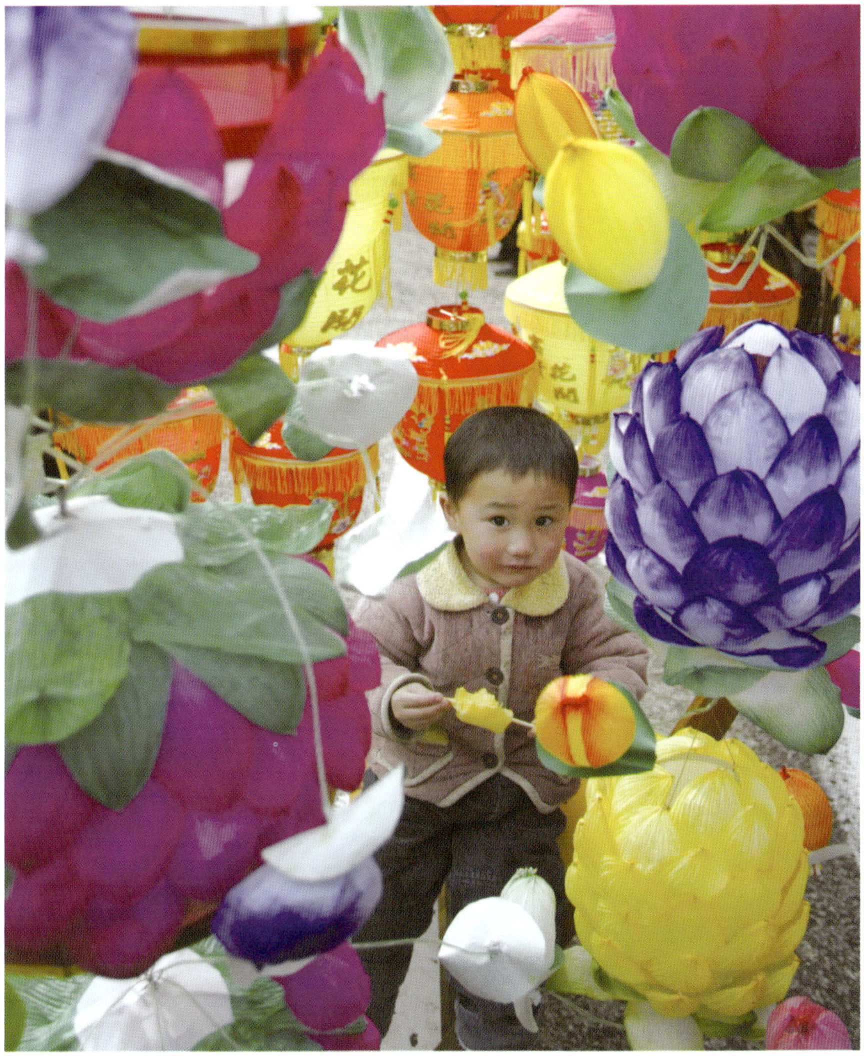

A variety of lanterns for the Lantern Festival

The game of lantern riddle guessing is held on the night of the Lantern Festival, a custom originating as far back as the seventh century BC during the Spring and Autumn Period—a time of frequent wars between kingdoms. In trying to convince the rulers

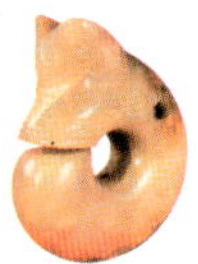

to adopt their ideas, advisors—rather than telling their kings what they should do—would use roundabout ideas to get their message across. Later, people started writing riddles on lanterns, with prizes for those who could answer correctly.

Food Served on the Lantern Festival

According to tradition, *yuan xiao* or *tang yuan* must be eaten on the day of the Lantern Festival. *Yuan xiao* consist of a glutinous rice flour wrap with a sweet filling—sugar, osmanthus, hawthorn, date paste, nuts, black sesame, plum, bean paste, coco are amongst the common materials—shaped into round balls, to symbolize togetherness and harmony of the family circle.

Legend has it that back in the Han Dynasty (206 BC-220 AD), Emperor Wudi's minister Dongfang Shuo was picking plum branches in the royal garden for the emperor, when he saw a palace maid by the name of Yuan Xiao, who was about to jump into a well and kill herself. Dongfang Shuo sympathized for this homesick girl and devised a stratagem whereby the girl would be able to see her family. He asked Yuan Xiao to be dressed in red and sent her to the streets of Chang'an, pretending to be a messenger sent by the god of fire. She told one and all that she was ordered to come to Chang'an to burn down the city and that even the Jade Emperor would watch her do so at the Southern Heavenly Gate. Everyone was scared. The girl in red told everyone that if they wanted to avoid this fire, a letter on red paper had to be delivered to the emperor soon. When Emperor

Wudi opened the letter, he read, "Chang'an is in peril. The
Imperial palace will be on fire. The fire will last sixteen days. Its
flames will make the night red."

Wudi was shocked and asked his minister for help. Dongfang
Shuo said that he knew that god of fire liked to eat *tang yuan* balls
and he knew that Yuan Xiao made the best *tang yuan*. Dongfang
Shuo suggested that on the fifteenth night of the first lunar month,

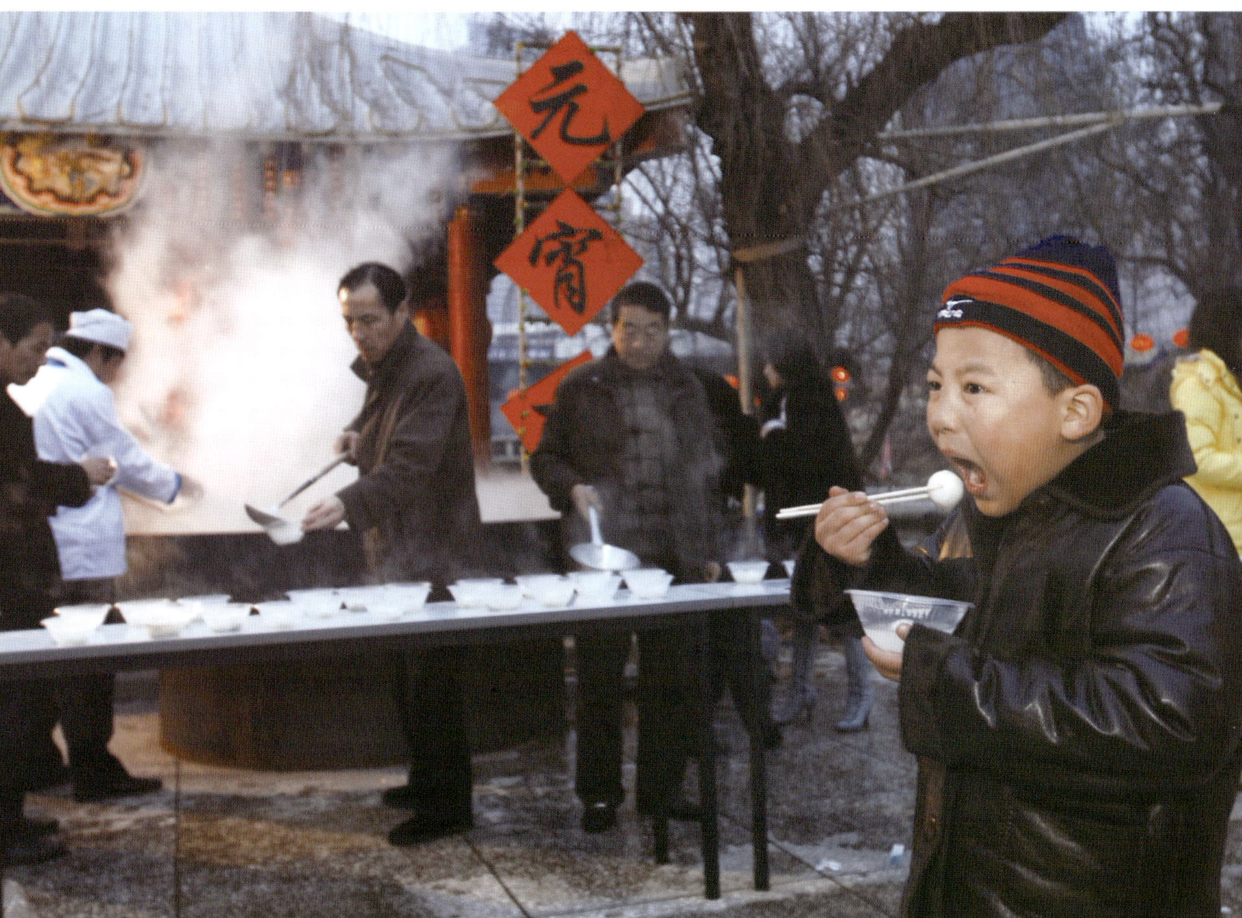

Eating sweet *yuanxiao* dumplings

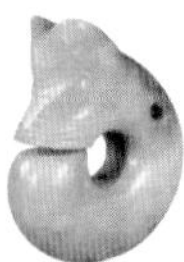

Yuan Xiao should make *tang yuan* for the god of fire and that every family should do likewise, so that the god might have a change of heart. Then, the following night, every household should hang lanterns outside their houses and in the streets and light firecrackers to make the city appear to be ablaze so that the Jade Emperor, standing at the Southern Heavenly Gate watching the city, might be fooled.

Emperor Wudi agreed to this idea. On the sixteenth night, when the city was lit up by lanterns and firecrackers Yuan Xiao's younger sister also came to watch lanterns with her parents. When she saw a big lantern bearing the words *yuan xiao*, she called out, "Sister Yuan Xiao!" When Yuan Xiao heard this, she appeared before her parents and sister. From then on, Yuan Xiao could always reunite with her family on this night.

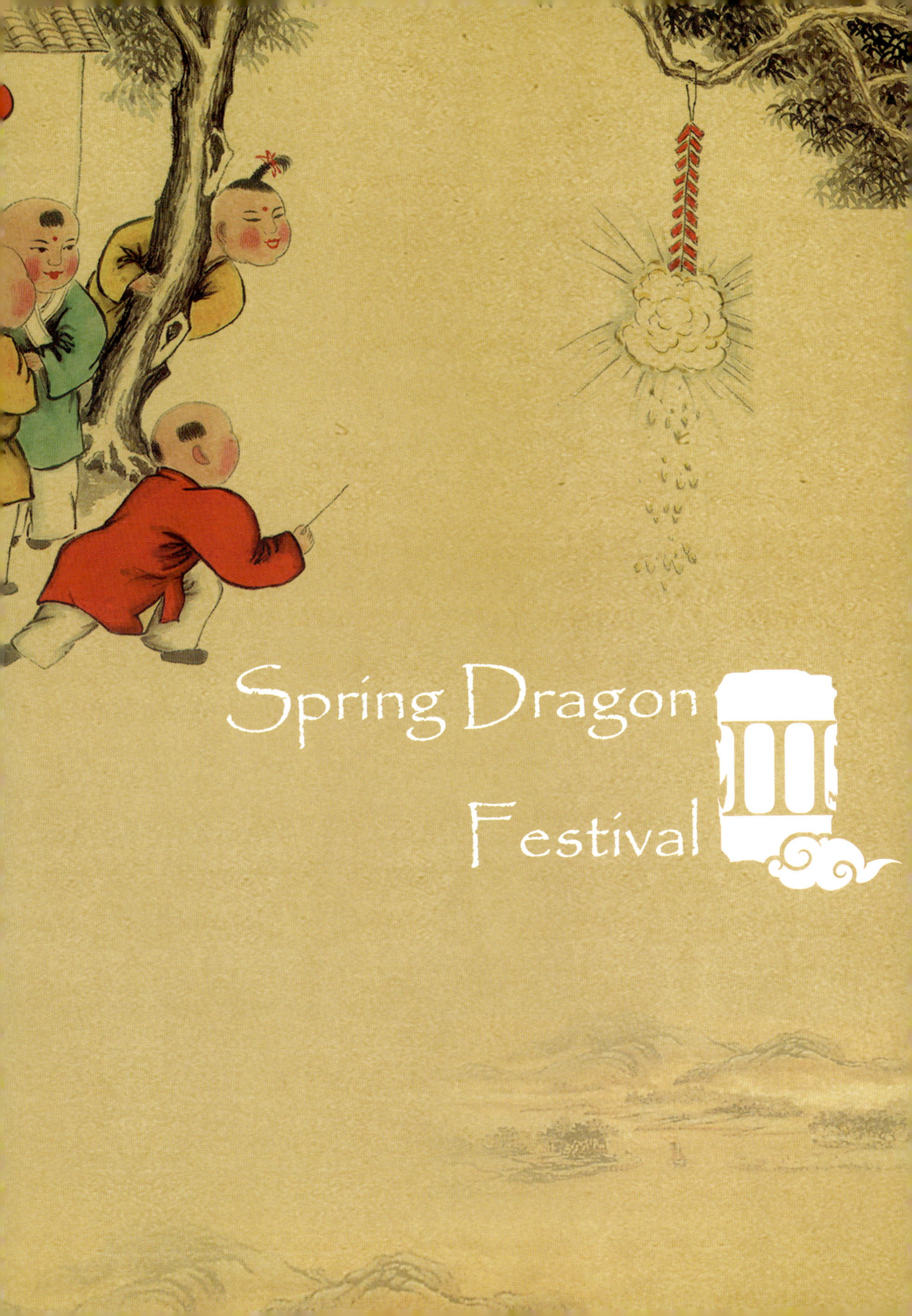
Spring Dragon Festival

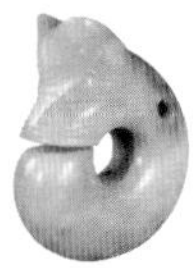

38

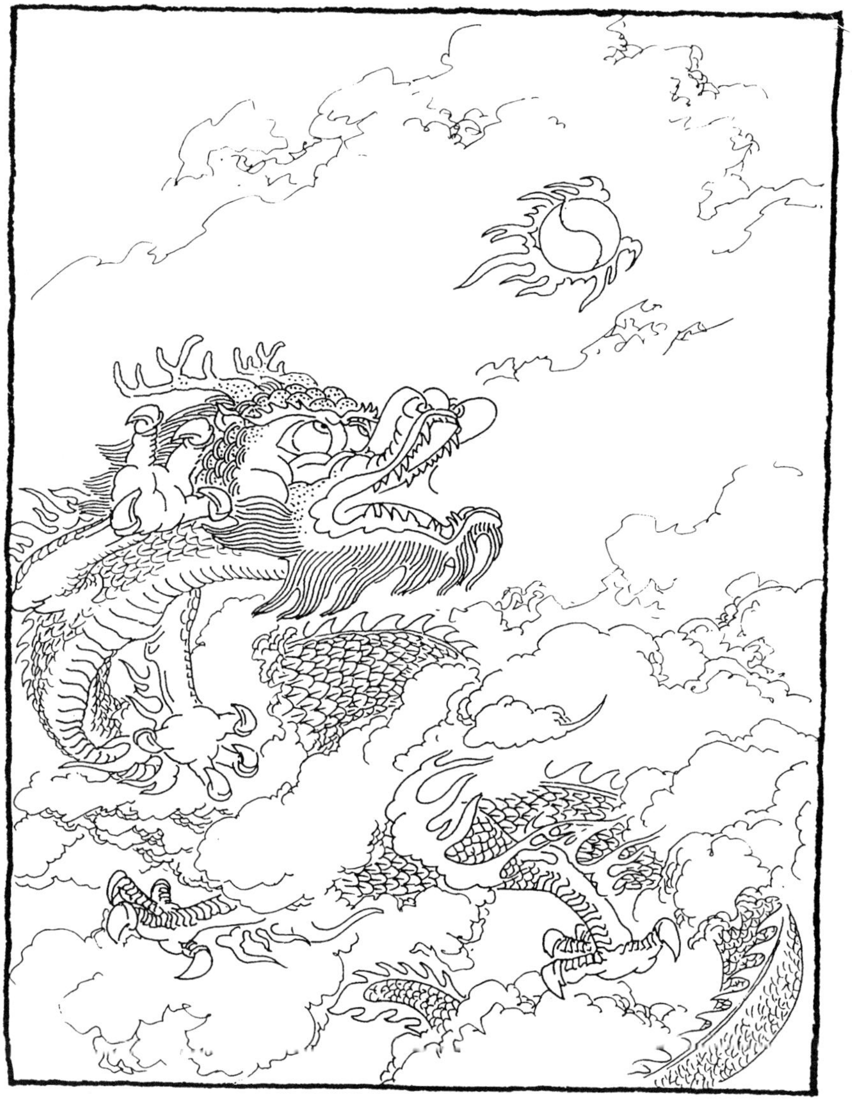

"The dragon raises its head on the second day of the second lunar month," thus beginning the Spring Dragon Festival. It is said the dragon wakes from its winter-long sleep on this day, roaring and shaking its tail, producing springtime thunder.

No one knows what a dragon looks like. Many archeologists believe there has never been such an animal as dragon existed on earth. But in Chinese folklore, this legendary animal is described as having the body of a snake, horns of a deer, talons of an eagle, face of a horse, two waving whiskers, all shimmering like gold. At the end of the primitive society, each tribe had its own totem with a distinct animal as its sign. That of the Xia tribe was a snake; that of the Shang was a bird. The tribes were constantly clashing and taking over each other. When the "snake" tribe defeated the "eagle" tribe, eagle talons would be added to the snake's body on its totem; when later it annexed the "deer" tribe, deer horns were added to the totem, and so on. Eventually, the dragon came into being.

The forms of dragons evolved over thousands of years. But there are two types of dragons in legend—the flying dragon and the coiling dragon. An ancient book said that Huang Di, one of the forefathers of the Chinese nation, ascended heaven by riding on a dragon more than 4,000 years ago. By the Tang and Song dynasties, temples were built in many places where people offered sacrifices and prayed to the dragon king for good weather for their crops. This tradition has been maintained until today. The coiling dragon comes from the story about Da Yu, a legendary king who succeeded in bringing the water under control and saved people from the catastrophe of floods. Da Yu is considered to be a descendant of the dragon. With the passage of time, dragons came to represent the highest authority, becoming symbols of emperors,

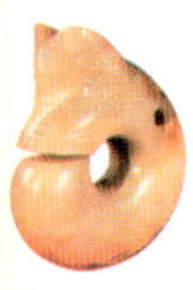

who called themselves "genuine dragon" or "son of heaven." A dragon was even embroidered on the flag of the Qing Dynasty.

Folk Customs at the Spring Dragon Festival

Customs vary from place to place. In the Shaanxi region of northwest China, women are not supposed to do needlework, for fear of hurting the dragon's eyes and provoking retaliation. Some would use ash or sugar to draw a snake or dragon, stretching all the way from the well to their home, in the hope of leading a dragon—and with it wealth—into their house. In Shandong and Jiangsu provinces, people would draw spiraling circles on the ground, symbolic of a barn, to predict a good harvest. Sometimes a ladder was drawn next to the circles to denote a barn piled high with grain.

As spring is also the time for pests to come out, people in some areas would make "scorpion's claws" by quick-frying soy beans with sugar; some would eat left-over sticky rice cake, believing it would make them strong and prevent them suffering back pain over a whole year's work in the fields; in some areas of Hunan, people would smear sticky stuff on tree branches and plant them in the field as bird-catchers to prevent them damaging the crops. In Fujian, this day was known as "walking the green" day, when people would go for walks in the countryside.

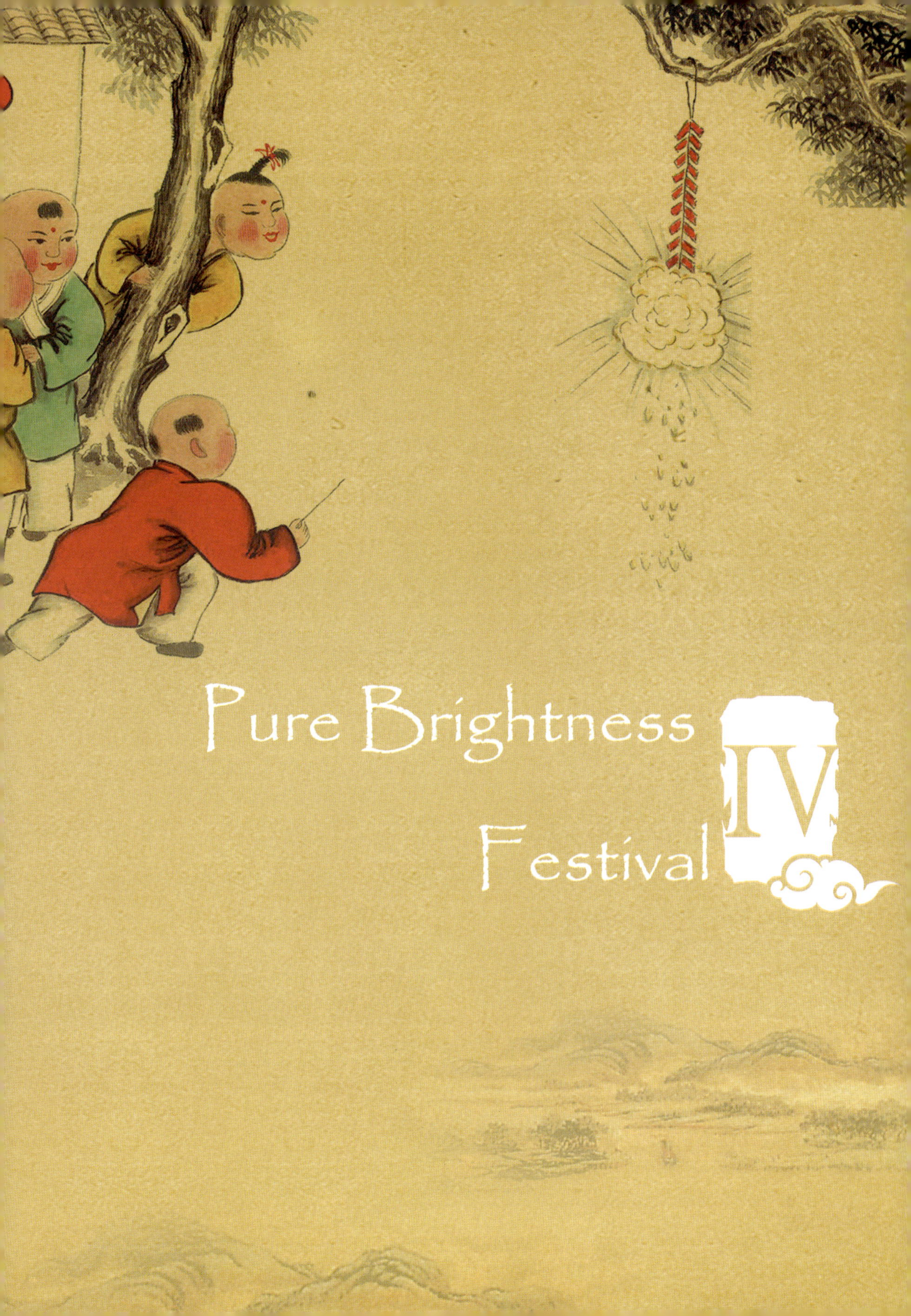

Pure Brightness
Festival
IV

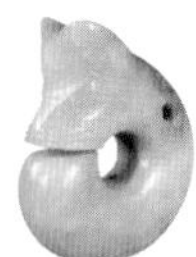

One of the most popular festivals in China, Pure Brightness Day falls on the 5th or 6th of April. On this day, people pay respects to the dead, go for a walk in the countryside or go sightseeing.

Pure Brightness Festival is also known as Cold Food Festival. Legend has it that in the Spring and Autumn Period over 2,000 years ago, Chong Er, son of the Duke of Jin, went into exile for 19 years, during which time many of his followers fled, unable to stand the hardships, leaving only five or six loyal followers, including Jie Zitui. When Chong Er had a desperate craving for meat, Jie Zitui cooked flesh from his own arm for Chong Er. Later when Chong Er took the throne that was rightfully his and became Duke Wen of Jin, he ennobled those followers who had been loyal to him in exile. But Jie Zitui and his mother decided that they would rather live in retreat than seek nobility and went to live in the Mian Mountain. The king was determined to find Jie Zitui, searching for him for days without success. He decided to smoke him out by setting fire to the mountain, and the fire burned for three days and nights. When the whole mountain was burned out, the king's search party found Jie Zitui and his mother holding onto a willow tree, burned to death. The king buried them at Mian Mountain, which he renamed Jie Mountain and established a temple in memory of his loyal follower. As a reminder of Jie Zitui's friendship, he had the willow tree taken from the mountain and had shoes made out of it.

The day that Duke Wen ordered the firing of the mountain happened to fall on Pure Brightness Day. To commend Jie Zitui's virtue of "preferring death to ennoblement," no family would cook on this day; only cold leftovers from the previous day were served. Also on this day, people would pay respect to their ancestors.

Customs on the Day of Pure Brightness

On this day, people go walking in the countryside or sightseeing. On their way home, women would make bonnets of willow twigs, indicating a wish to remain forever young, since there was a belief that "Without a willow bonnet on the hair, the tender face becomes a white head." The Tang Dynasty poet Du Mu, describing the scene on this day, wrote: "Drizzling rain on the Day of Pure Brightness; people on the road seem to have lost their soul. Asked is there an inn nearby, the cowherd boy points to Apricot Blossom Village." The custom of paying respect to one's ancestors is still practiced today.

Kites

Popular sports activities during the Festival of Pure Brightness included playing on swings, kicking ball, cock fighting, dog walking and kite flying.

Kite flying dates back over 2,000 years, to the Spring and Autumn Period when a man by the name of Gong Shuban made a wooden hawk and had it fly high up in the sky in order to get information about an enemy state. Later paper was used to make the paper hawk. Han Xin (?-196 BC), a military strategist of

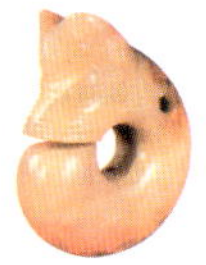

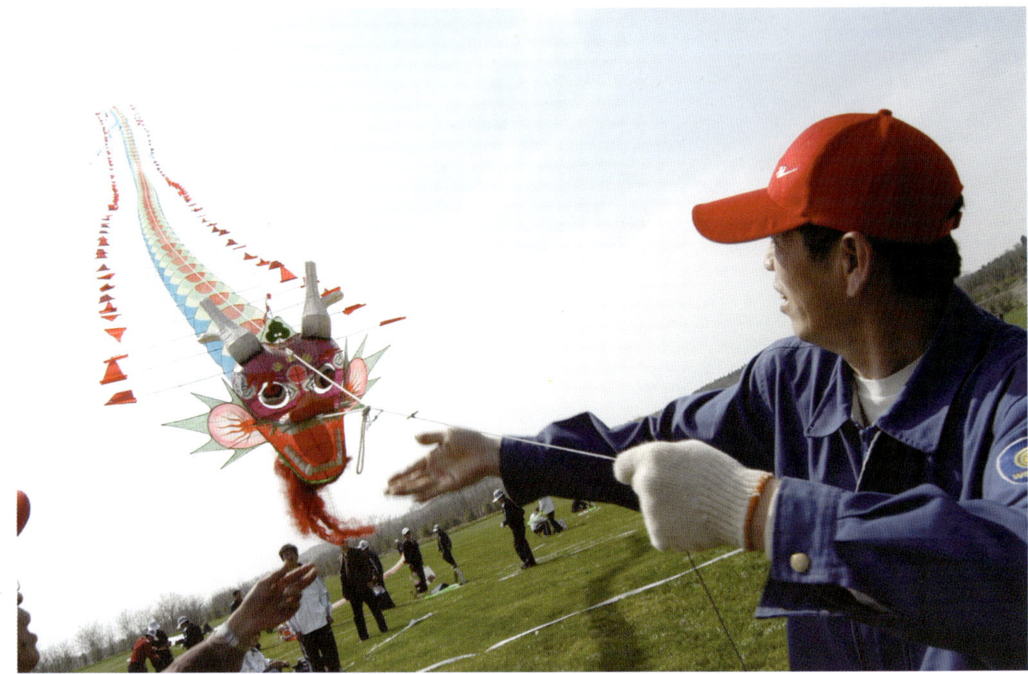

the Western Han Dynasty, is believed to be inventor of the paper hawk, or kite. Kites were first used for military purposes and appeared in ancient battlefields.

By the 10th century AD, a man named Li Bei attached to the kite a bamboo pipe or silk thread, not only for flying but also making a whistling sound in flight.

The use of kites for pleasure brought about development in their forms. There are kites in the shape of legendary heavenly gods, local opera characters, colorful butterflies, goldfish with beautiful flying tails, dragonflies, birds, bats, eagles, frogs and centipedes. Every year around spring, people go out flying their kites. These works of traditional Chinese arts and crafts enjoy a high worldwide reputation.

Currently in the collection of the Palace Museum in Beijing, *Scenes on the River during the Festival of Pure Brightness*, a horizontal scroll painting by Zhang Zeduan, a 12th century artist of the Northern Song Dynasty, is the most outstanding realistic painting in China's fine art

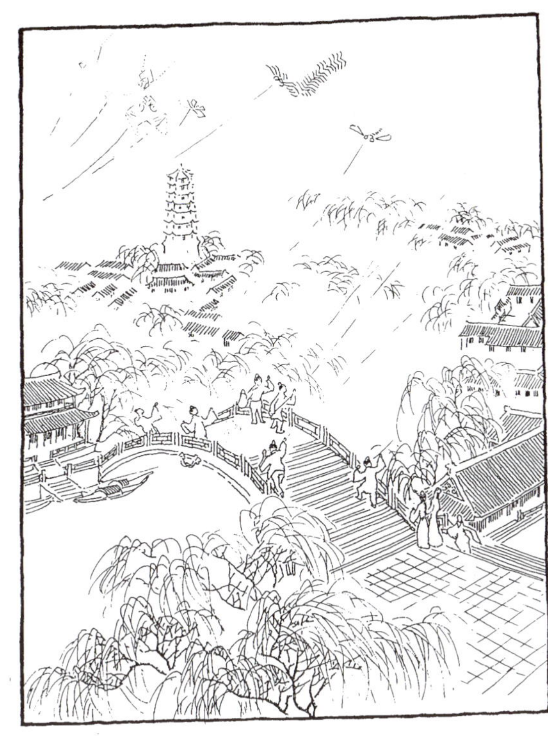

An ancient painting of kite-flying during the Pure Brightness Festival

history. It vividly depicts scenes of life in Bianliang (today's Kaifeng), capital of the Northern Song, during the Festival of Pure Brightness. The scroll starts with a small group paying respects at their ancestors' tombs, with budding willow trees on both sides of the Bian River. In the distance can be seen horses and mules deep in the woods. Laborers taking a break by the roadside and farmers working in the field are also vividly shown. As the river becomes wider, more pedestrians, boats, boat trackers can be seen; there are people working on ships at the quays; on the bridges are people looking down at the river. The city streets are full of teahouses, inns, restaurants and shops. Mounted officials are carried on horseback, ladies in sedan chairs; there are civilians and laborers. The scroll has altogether 1,643 figures, 208 animals, 20-odd vehicles and boats, and 30-plus houses of

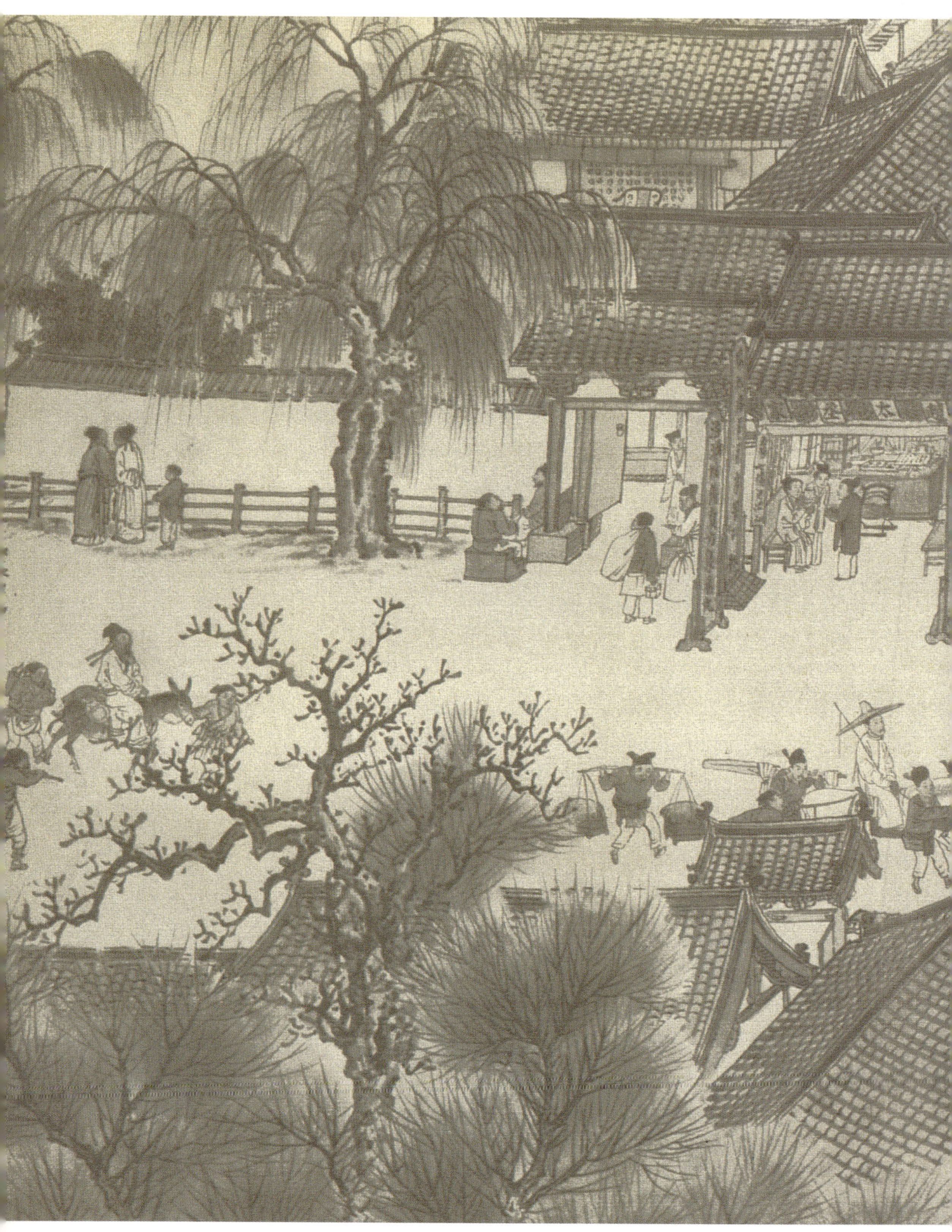

The famous painting *Scenes on the River during the Festival of Pure Brightness* by a 12th century artist

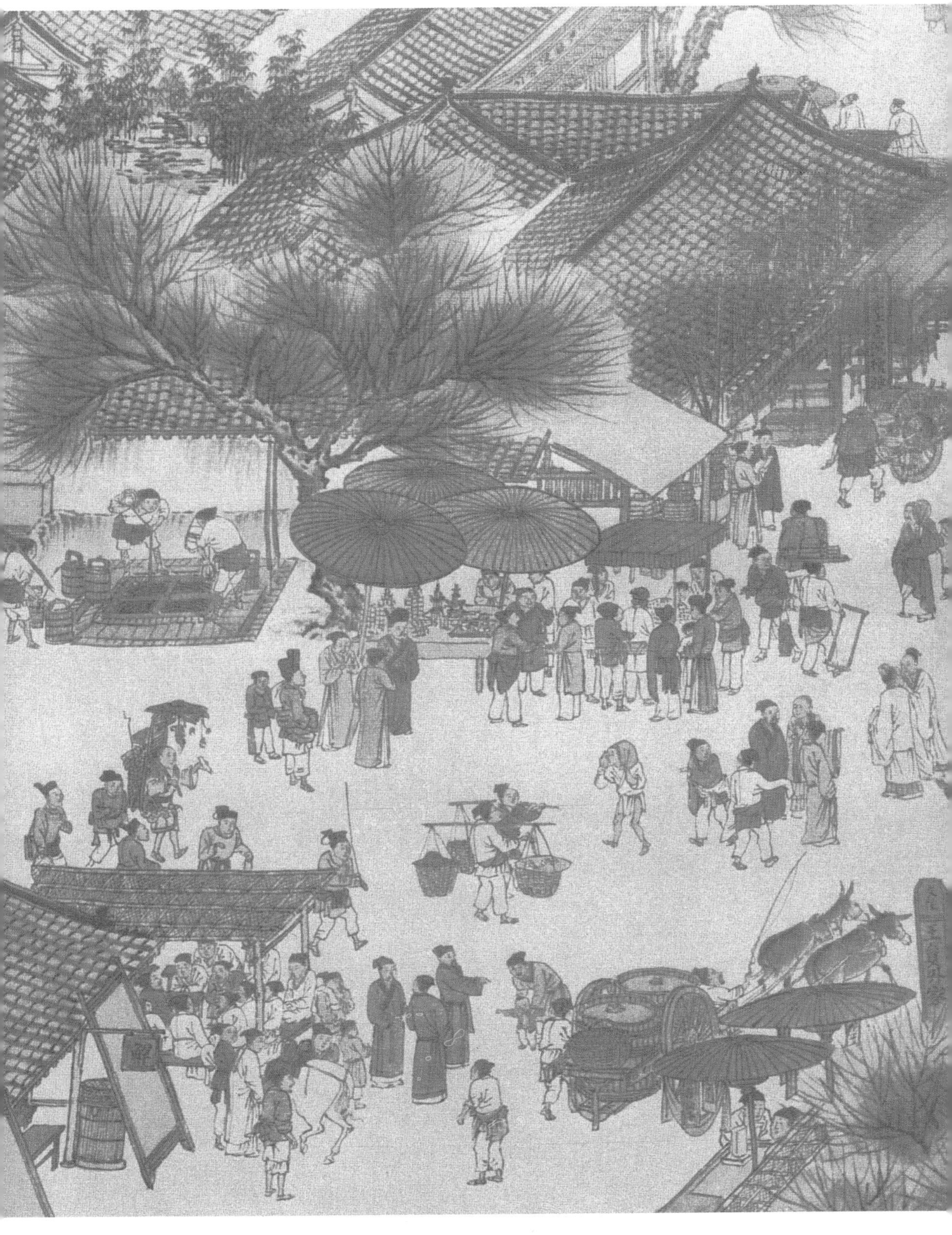

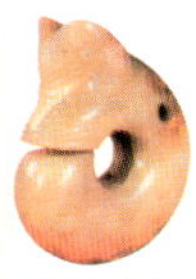

every kind. The painting is a vivid portrayal of the lives of people from all social classes and of the prosperity of the Northern Song capital.

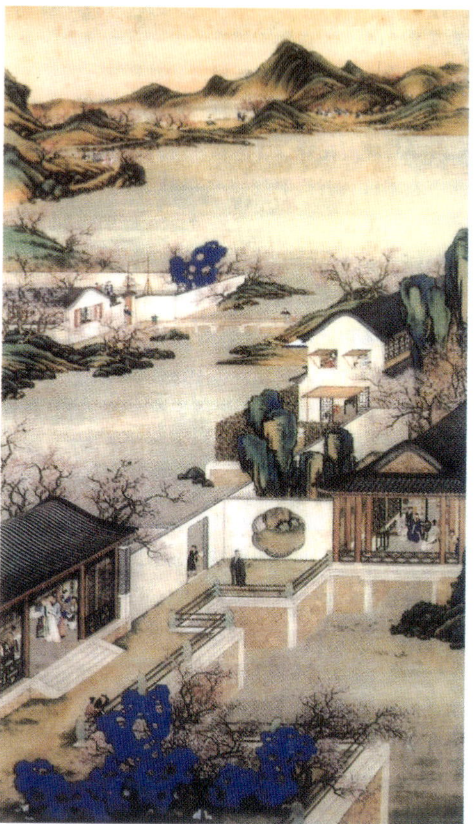

A walk in the countryside in spring

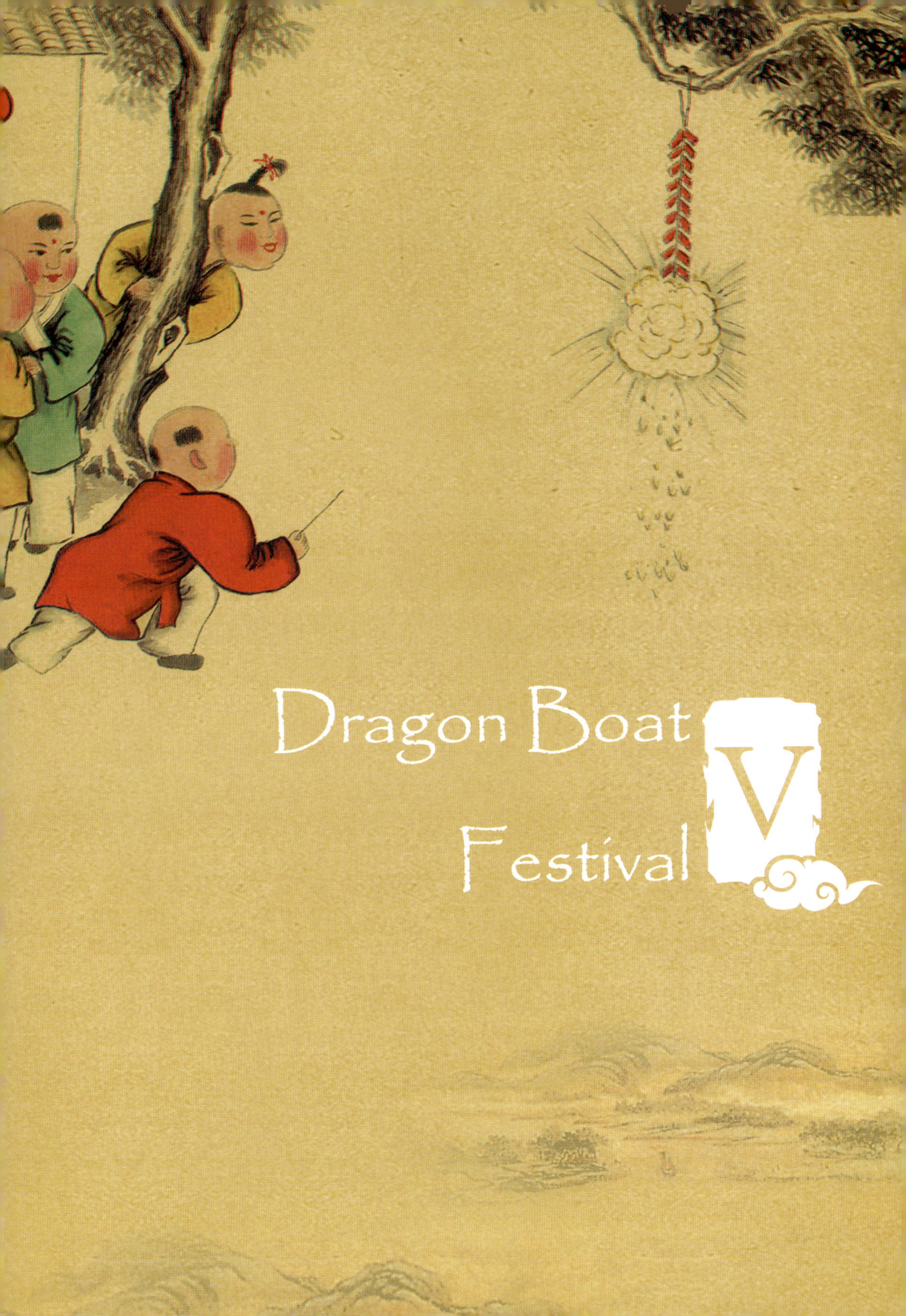
Dragon Boat
Festival
V

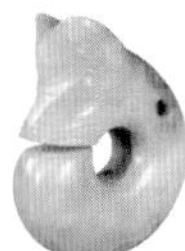

One of China's three major folk festivals, the Dragon Boat Festival falls on the fifth day of the fifth lunar month. According to the renowned modern scholar Wen Yiduo, this festival was in existence as long as 2,500 years ago and because it had much to do with dragons, he concluded that "Dragon Boat Festival was a day for totem sacrifice held by the dragon totem tribe; in short it was a dragon festival." Pottery and stone wares with geometric prints dating back to between the late Neolithic Period and second century B.C. that have been excavated recently in southern provinces such as Guangdong, Guangxi, Fujian, Taiwan, Zhejiang, Jiangsu, Anhui, Hunan and Hubei—judging from historical legend and geographical features—seem to belong to a group known as Baiyue, a totem worshipping tribe. They practiced the folk custom of "hair cutting and tattooing to resemble the offspring of a dragon." They called themselves descendants of the dragon so this festival was both their own festival as well as that of the dragon. After the disappearance of totem culture, the old practice of dragon tattoos evolved beyond body tattoos and into the dragon boat ceremony. The practice of eating *zongzi* dumplings, containing sticky rice in a pyramid-shaped wrap of bamboo or reed leaves, was meant to commemorate the dragon. Some places have the custom of collecting rainwater on this day because of a belief that rain falling on this day was sacred water spread to the earth by the heavenly dragon, and that it would eliminate disasters and cure diseases. In the past in some other places, a coiling dragon was cast into the middle of a river as a plea for rain. With the passing of totem culture, the dragon festival no longer had any

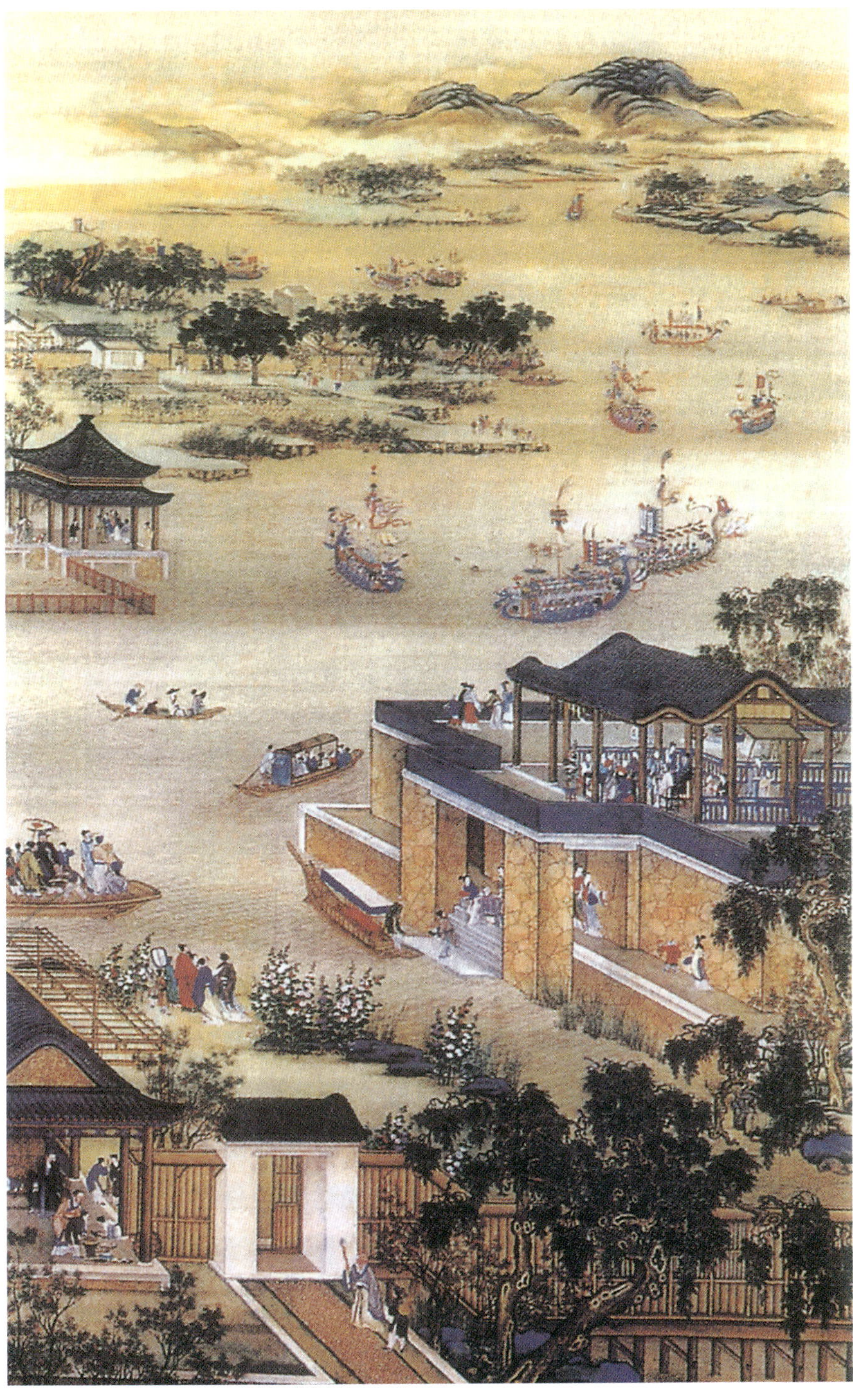

A dragon-boat race in commemoration of Qu Yuan

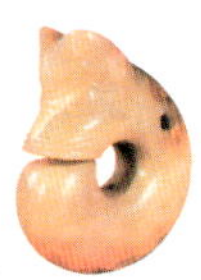

meaning in terms of totem worship and attached itself to the story of the patriotic poet Qu Yuan.

The Day In Memory of Qu Yuan

The common belief that the Dragon Boat Festival commemorates the poet Qu Yuan has been accepted in practice; and indeed there is some truth in this account of its origin.

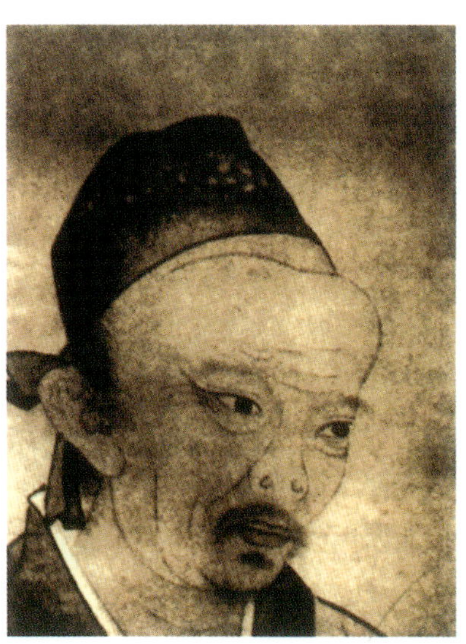

An image of Qu Yuan

Born in 340 B.C., Qu Yuan was a patriotic poet living in the state of Chu during the Warring States Period. Faced with the corruption of the Chu nobility, Qu Yuan proposed cabinet reform, establishment of a legal system and appointment by ability. However, corrupt officials opposed his progressive ideas and he was forced into exile.

Qu Yuan, over 50 years old and beset by grief, left the Chu capital and wandered in Xiapu and Lingyang. It was during this time that he wrote *Li Sao*, his famous long poem of patriotism, *Nine Songs*, and *Nine Chapters*. In 278 B.C., the army of Qin captured the Chu capital. As his country faced downfall, the 62-year-old Qu Yuan jumped into the Miluo River weighted down by a rock, laying down his life for Chu.

Qu Yuan's noble spirit of sacrificing his own life for his ideal won the respect of the people. On hearing the news, people everywhere came to the river and rowed out in search of his body. He was not found. "The Chu people felt sad. Every year on this day, people would put rice into bamboo tubes and throw them into the river in memory of him." This was said to be the origin of Dragon Boat Festival activities such as rowing dragon boats and eating *zongzi* dumplings. The practice of planting mugwort and calamus leaves was also supposed to call back the spirit of Qu Yuan.

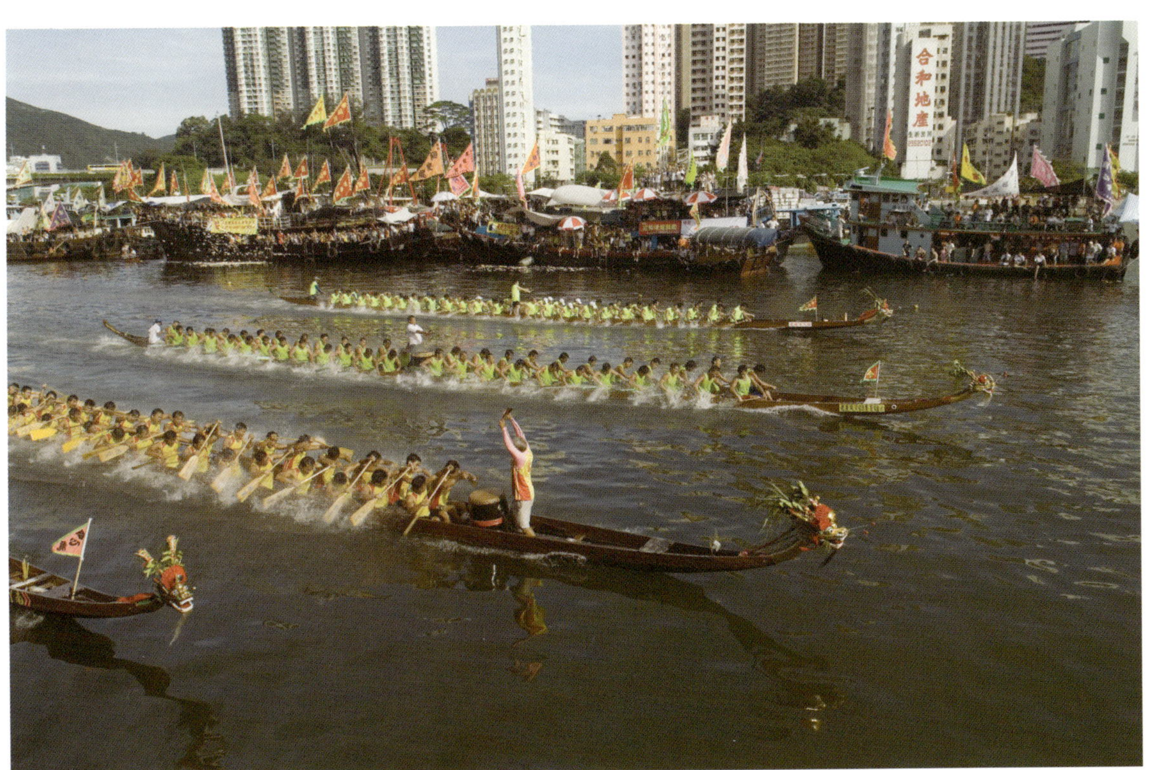

One can't celebrate the Dragon Boat Festival without having a dragon-boat race, a tradition that has continued for hundreds of years.

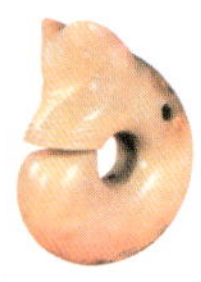

Zongzi Dumplings

Zongzi dumplings are essential at Dragon Boat Festival. Legend has it that during the Jianwu period (25-56 AD) of the Western Han Dynasty, a man by the name of Ou Hui saw a man introducing himself as a *san lu* official, a position Qu Yuan used to hold. This man told Ou Hui that he was glad that people mourned him, but that most of the sacrificial food was eaten by the dragon in the river. He suggested to Ou Hui that, in future, the rice should be wrapped in leaves and tied with colorful threads, two things that the dragon feared, so that it would no longer dare steal the food. Later people took his suggestion and *zongzi* came into being.

According to the *Record of Folk Customs*, a book written in the Jin Dynasty (second to fourth century AD), millet was wrapped in wild rice leaves and boiled until very soft, to be enjoyed on the fifth day of the fifth month. During the Tang and Song dynasties, *zongzi* appeared in many varieties and shapes involving ingredients such as dates and sugar, with the addition sometimes of pine nuts, chestnuts, walnuts, cinnamon

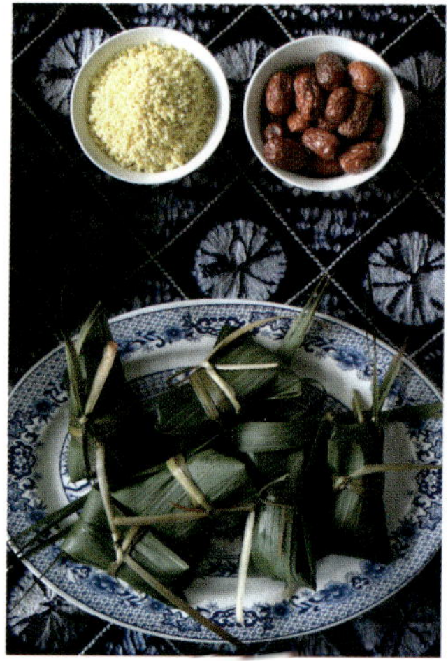

zongzi

and even musk. By the Ming Dynasty, glutinous rice was being used, together with dates, chestnuts, dried persimmon, gingko nuts and red beans. The famous mugwort-flavored *zongzi* was so named because rice was soaked together with mugwort leaves. In the Qing Dynasty palace, cheese was used to soak the rice overnight before the rice was wrapped in leaves and boiled. In the south of China, the most famous *zongzi* were the ham variety. Mini-*zongzi* were deep fried and known as "food of the immortals." The fillings for *zongzi*, in addition to dates and sugar, included all kinds of ingredients—red bean paste, preserved fruit, nuts, rock sugar, yam, hawthorn fruit and sesame seeds, for example.

The *zongzi* from Jiaxing in Zhejiang Province are the most particular in their ingredients. Ham is cut into small pieces and marinaded with sugar, wine and salt. A slice of fat pork is sandwiched between two slices of lean so when the *zongzi* are done, the rice tastes tender and soft, but not greasy. Cantonese *zongzi* have a lotus leaf wrap, their fillings involving salty duck eggs, chicken, duck, pork, mushrooms and green bean paste. They are much bigger too, some weighing as much as a pound apiece. *Zongzi* made of glutinous millet is among the most popular types of *zongzi* in North China.

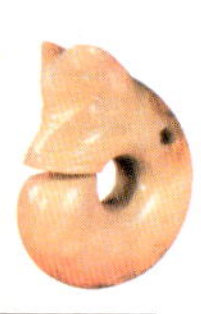

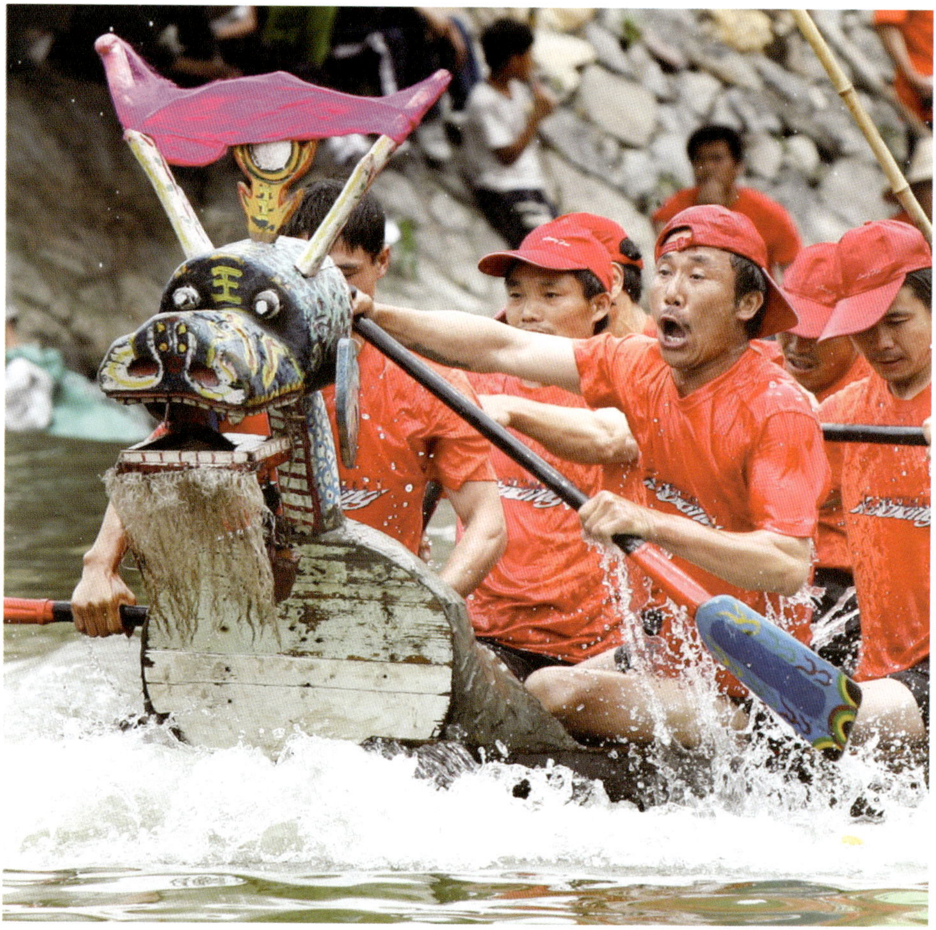

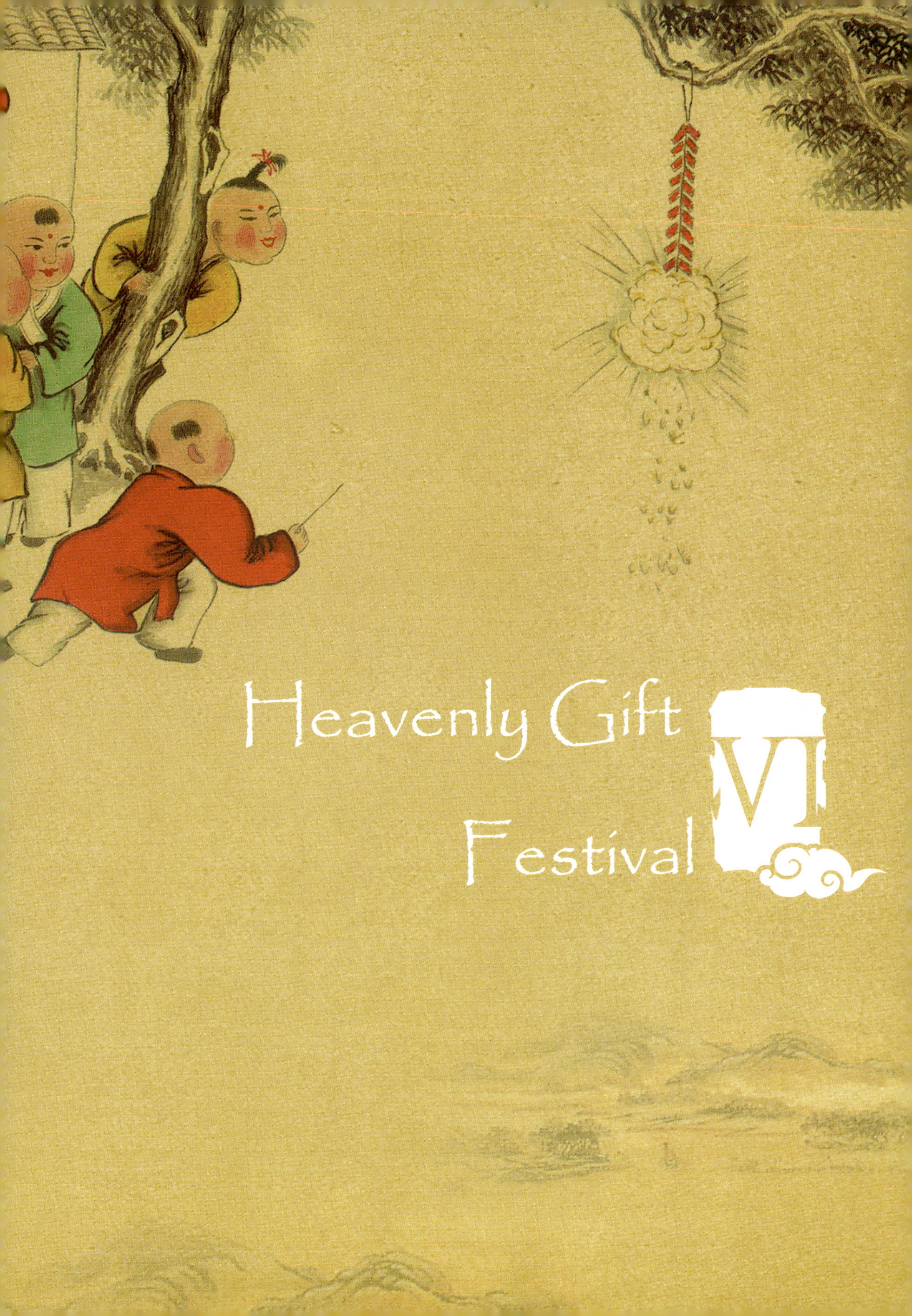
Heavenly Gift
Festival
VI

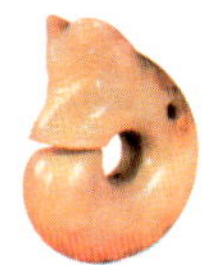

Origin of Heavenly Gift Festival

This festival used to be celebrated every year on the sixth day of the sixth month. According to legend, in 219 BC, after the First Emperor of Qin had unified all China, he went to sacred Mount Tai in Shandong Province. Here at the Dai Temple— later known as Heavenly Gift Hall—he worshipped heaven and asked to be granted the supreme mandate. Emperors of following dynasties followed his example. On this day, they too would climb Mount Tai to worship heaven and to ask for the supreme mandate, naming themselves "heavenly son of the genuine dragon." Over the years, the Heavenly Gift Hall underwent many renovations and the sixth day of the sixth month became a festival date. The Song Emperor Zhenzong (968-1022) falsely claimed that a heavenly book would fall from heaven on the sixth day of the sixth month in a certain year. If a wise monarch obtained this book and governed in accordance with heaven's will, the world would be at peace, the country would be strong and people would become rich.

But Buddhism offers a different explanation. It was said that the Monk Xuanzang, who made the perilous pilgrimage to India to obtain true Buddhist scriptures, somehow got them wet during his return journey, and that it was only because he managed to dry them out that we have them today. Buddhist monks in Zhejiang Province used to air their scriptures, and this later became the practice of chanting scriptures. On the fifth night of the sixth month, groups of believers would come to the temples to chant scriptures.

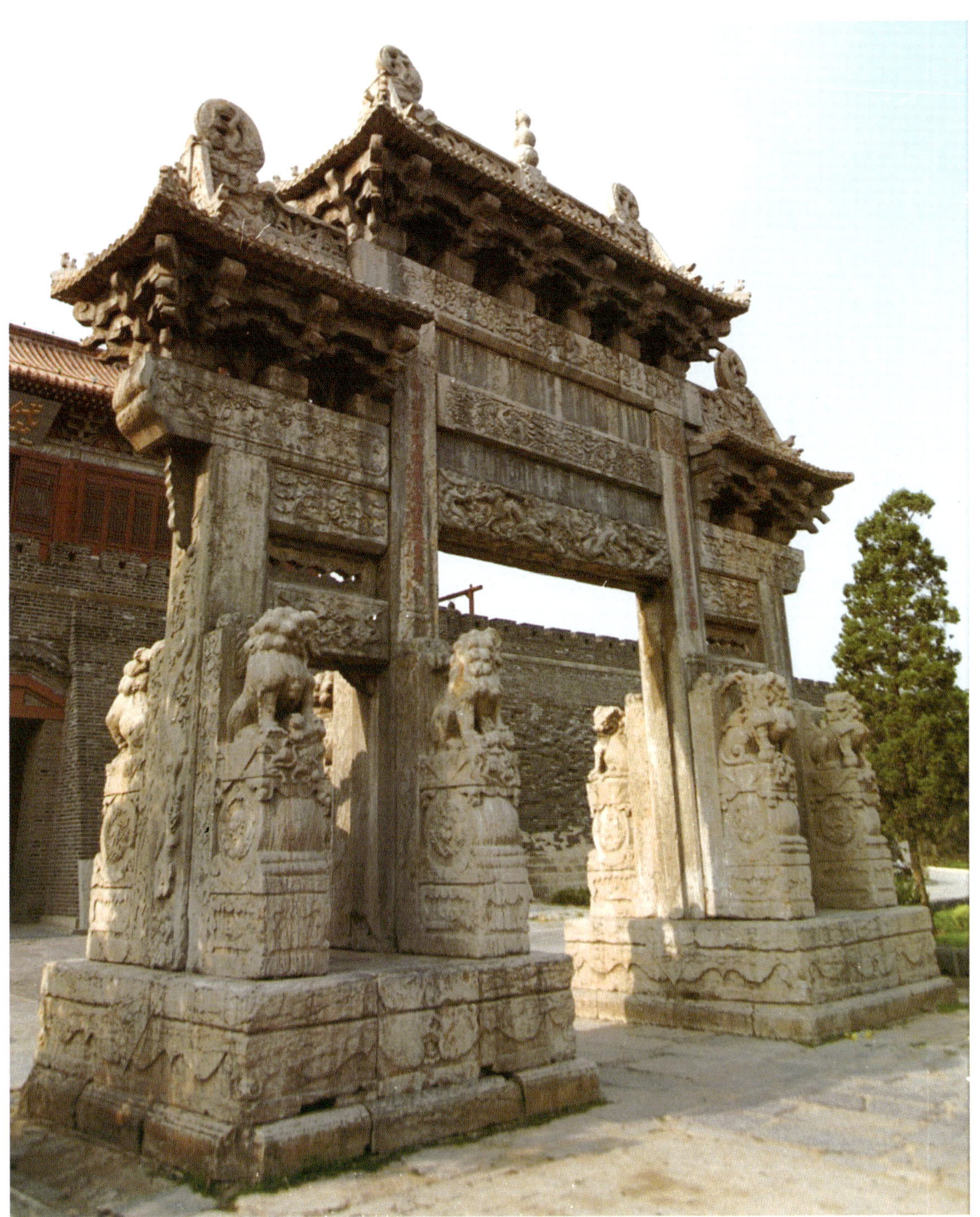

The Dai Temple

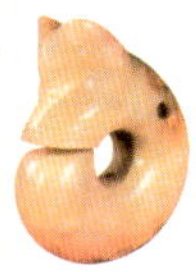

60

Customs at Heavenly Gift Festival

On this day, people in Shandong Province would stir wheat flour in a hot wok, then adding hot water, sugar or salt to make it into flour mush, which was believed to prevent diarrhea. In Hebei Province, people would store water on this day because it was believed that water on the sixth day of the sixth month was the best for making liquor.

In many other places, people would air their clothes, quilts and books on the sixth day of the sixth month, which happened to be the hottest day of summer. Some call airing clothes "airing dragon robes." In addition to this practice, people in Hunan Province would also warm water under the sun and bathe their children in it on this day.

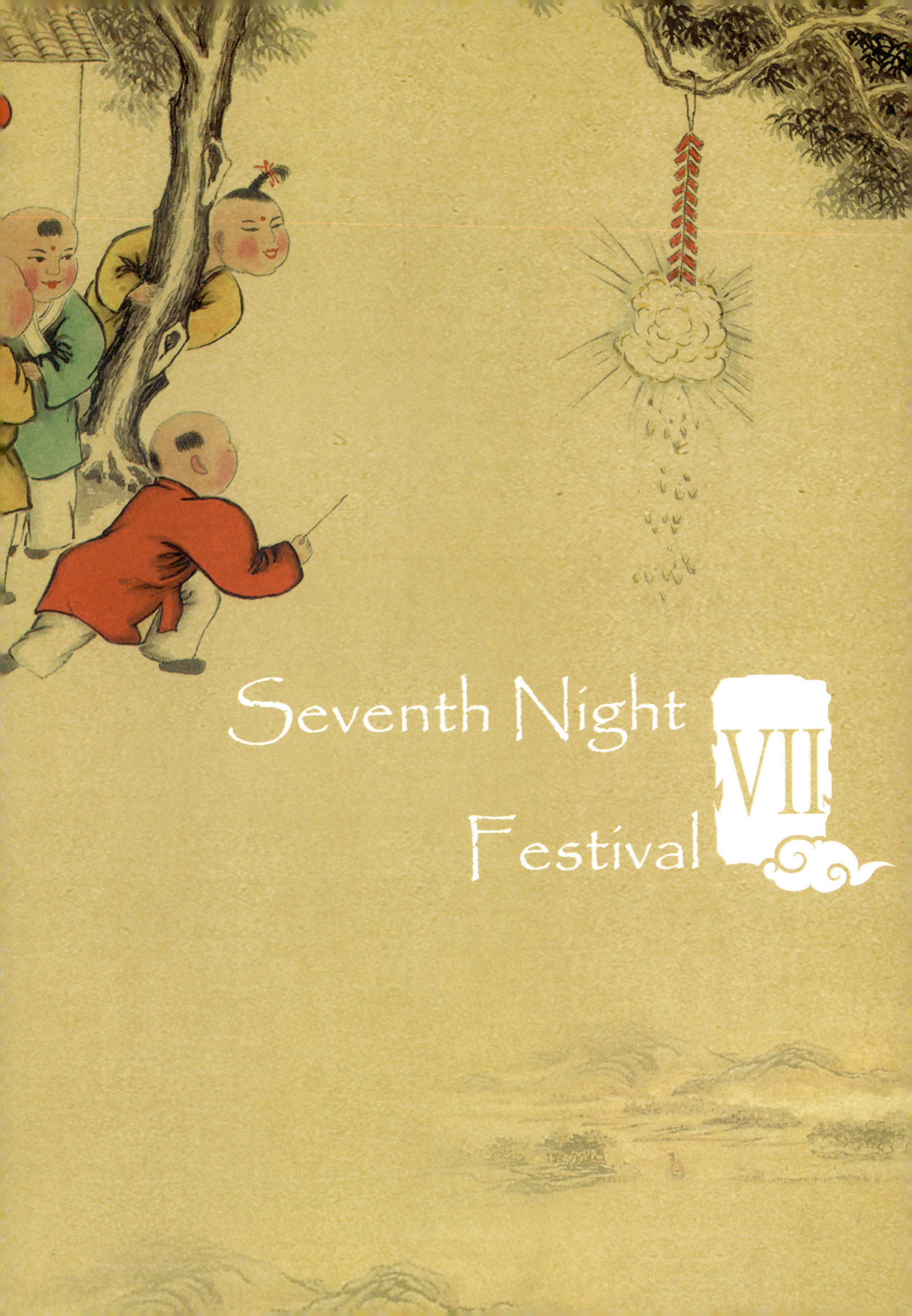
Seventh Night
Festival
VII

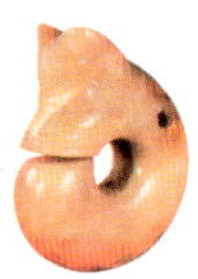

The seventh night of the seventh month of the lunar calendar is known as the "Seventh Night," and celebrates a moving love story.

The Cowherd and the Weaver Maid

The Cowherd was an honest and hard-working orphan boy, whose parents died when he was young. He went to live with his brother's family, but his brother's nasty wife drove him

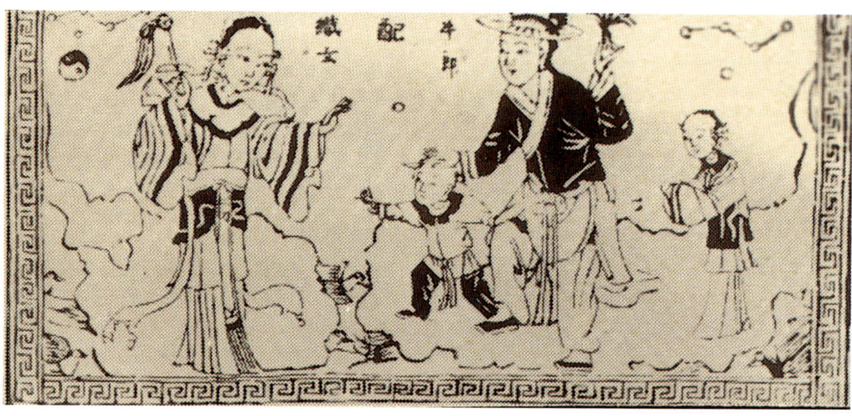

A picture of the Cowherd and the Weaver Maid

out. When the Cowherd left, he was given an ox, an old cart and some land. The Cowherd and his ox "Big Brother Ox" depended on each other for survival. The ox, wanting to see Cowherd happy and married, told his human friend that that on a certain day, seven fairy maidens would come down to earth to bathe and that if he could find a robe of one of the maidens, that maiden would be his wife. The Cowherd did as he was bid and succeeded one night in getting the robe of the Weaver Maid. They married and lived together happily for three years, raising a son and a daughter. When the god of heaven learned about this, he sent his wife to bring the Weaver Maid back to stand trial at the heavenly court, thus separating the loving couple. Downcast, the ox broke off his own horn to fashion a boat, taking the Cowherd and children in pursuit of the Weaver Maid. He had almost caught up when the wife of the god of heaven pulled out a hairpin and drew a river in the sky, blocking their way. Thus separated, the Cowherd and Weaver Maid could only see each other from a distance. A kindly phoenix, touched by their love, called all the magpies under heaven and asked them to build a bridge over this celestial river. Eventually, the couple met each other on the seventh night. It was said that on this night, countless feathers would fall from the sky because of all the magpies flying to build the bridge enabling the loving couple to meet.

If you see shining white air in the sky on this day, it means that the Weaver Maid is crossing the river. People believe that only the very lucky can see this scene. If you get on your knees and ask for wealth, longevity and a son, you will get one of the three within three years. They say that when the Weaver Girl crosses the river the gates of heaven will open immediately, and that if you throw a clay brick to the sky, a gold brick will fall.

Begging for Dexterity

The Weaver Maid was said to be very good at weaving and the festival is also known as the Festival of Begging for Dexterity— i.e. that the Weaver Maid would pass on her skills. In the distant

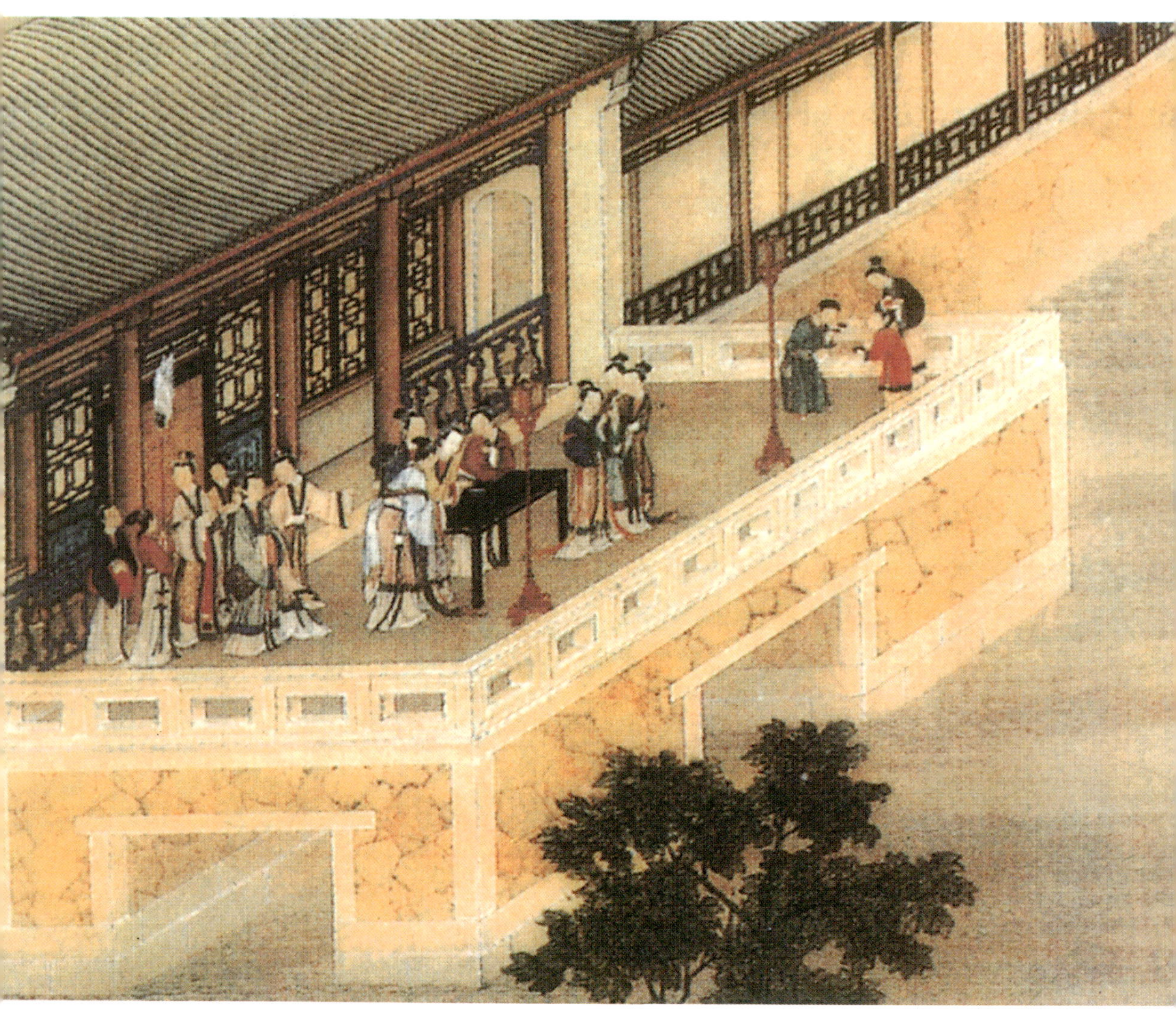

Activities in the imperial court to "beg for dexterity" on the Seventh Night Festival

past, there were two ways of begging for dexterity—prediction and soaking. The prediction method involved a girl putting a small spider in a box and opening it up the next day to see what web the spider had woven; a close and well-rounded web meant that she would get weaving dexterity. Soaking involved soaking a green bean or pea in water in the sixth month and changing the water every few days. By the seventh day of the seventh month, when the sprout was about a foot long, a red paper ribbon would be tied around the middle of the sprout. After worshipping the Cowherd and Weaver Maid, the girl would break the tip of the sprout into several pieces and throw them into a basin of clear water. Before the sunrise the next morning, if the reflection at the bottom of the basin showed the shadow of fine needle-like sprouts, she was said to have obtained dexterity. It was said that if a girl could hear the Cowherd and Weaver Maid whispering in the deep of the night, she was believed to have received dexterity. In some areas, the Seventh Night was also known as Girl's Day. On this night, girls would gather to worship the stars of the Cowherd and Weaver Maid (Altair and Vega) and compete at threading colorful threads through a nine-hole needle.

Seventh Night in Poetry

The Cowherd and Weaver Maid legend has touched many men of letters and poems about the two abound. *Star of the Cowherd Far, Far Away* is the earliest and most popular ancient poem: "Separated by the Milky Way, Weaver Maid and Cowherd

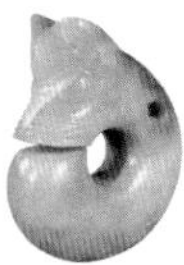

yearn for each other; waving her slender hands, her shuttle never stops weaving the cloth. No matter how hard she toils, still she is unable to make beautiful silk, for she feels so sad and her tears flow like a river. To see her lover, who knows how far she has to travel?" *Fairy over the Magpie Bridge—Tricks of the Soft Clouds* by the Song poet Qin Guan is a fine poem in praise of everlasting love: "Patches of colorful clouds cleverly change their shapes. From each side of the Milky Way, Cowherd and Weaver Maid tell each other how they hate to be apart. Though able to meet only at night after crossing the wide Milky Way, their meeting is still sweeter than any rendezvous in the human world. Love feels as soft as water and time together feels like a dream. When the time arrives to say goodbye, it breaks their hearts to tread the Magpie Bridge, the way back to their own separate homes. So long as there is mutual love, why stay together day in, day out?"

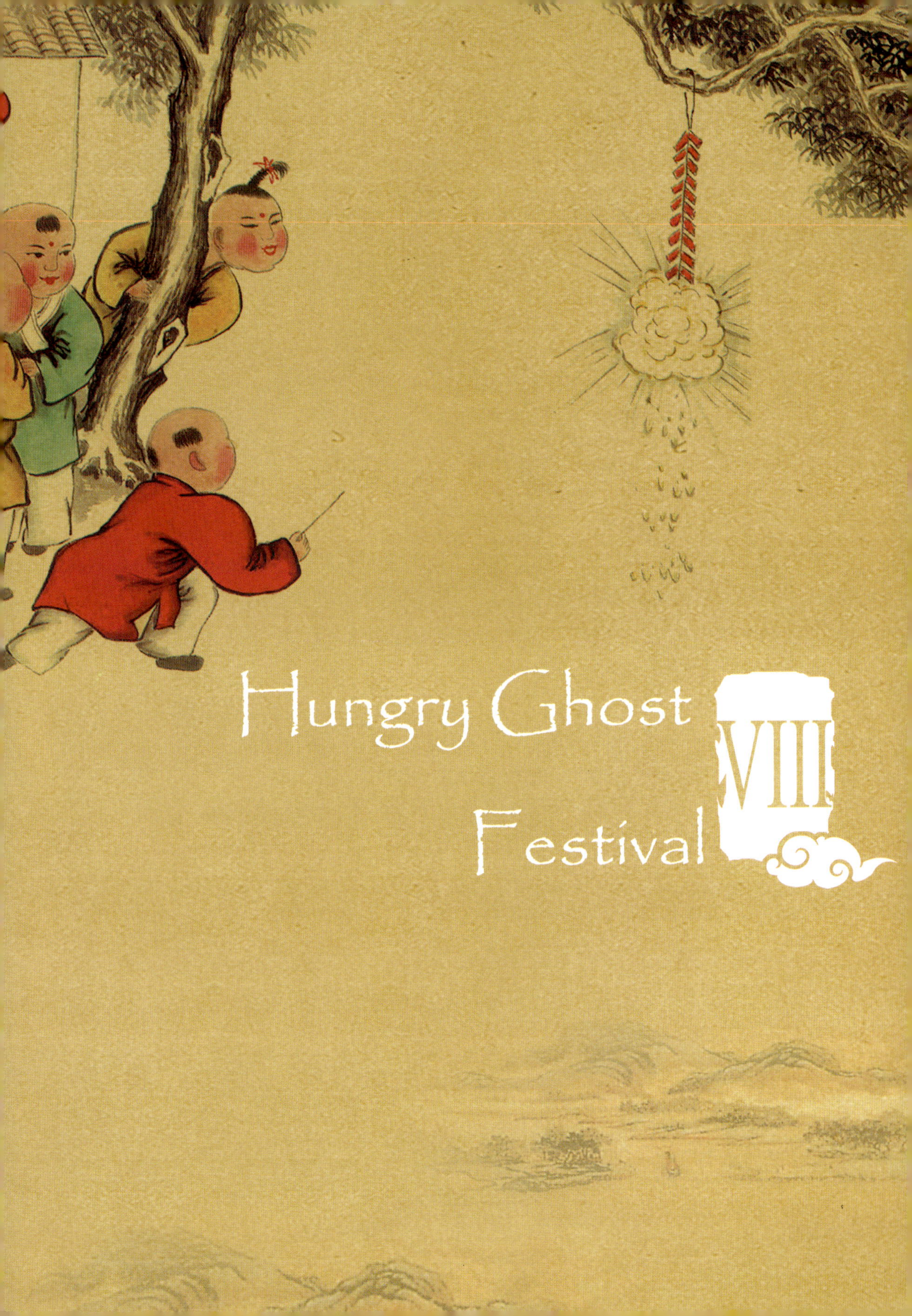
Hungry Ghost
Festival
VIII

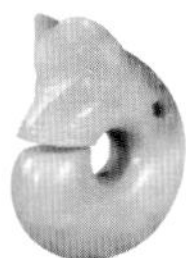

The Hungry Ghost Festival, falling on the 15th day of the seventh lunar month, is a Buddhist holiday.

One of the several versions of how this festival originated says that Sakyamuni, the founder of Buddhism, was reincarnated in the belly of Madame Moye of the Pure Stem Kingdom. Another has it that officials from the netherworld would come to earth on this day and judge who had done good or evil, and all the sufferers in the netherworld could be saved only when Taoists were invited to chant Buddhist scriptures from morning till night. However, the more common story describes how Mulian (the arhat Maudgalyayana) saved his mother, who died and fell into the realm of hungry ghosts, where whatever food she ate was transformed into fire. In order to save his mother, Mulian asked Buddha for help. Buddha gave him a set of the Dire Predicament Sutra and told him that chanting it would summon deities from all over to rescue his mother from her suffering. Thus, on 15th day of the seventh lunar month, Mulian chanted this sutra.

Because of this story, rich Buddhists started to practice filial piety, which they believed was the first of all merits. Around the 15th of the seventh month, they would ask monks and nuns to chant sutras—the Dire Predicament Sutra, in most cases— and to pray for them; at the same time, incense was burned and food sacrificed in memory of their parents, even to ancestors of seven generations back. They would also give alms to the monks and nuns to repay the kindness of their parents for raising them. As on the Day of Pure Brightness, many would go to the tombs and pay respects to their deceased ancestors on the 15th day of the seventh month. Because people also chanted scriptures and offered sacrifices to hungry ghosts and lonely souls on this day, it was known as the Ghost Festival.

Gradually the sutra chanting ritual evolved into a fair. During the day, sutras were chanted and lamps were floated onto rivers at night. During the Ming Dynasty in southern China, 36 lamps would be lit on the river this night. People believed that the drifting lamps could release these lonely souls from suffering. In

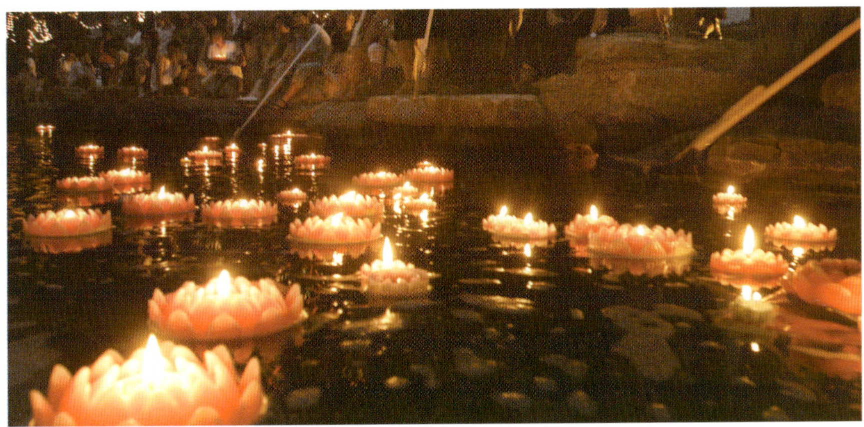

Floating lotus-shaped lamps onto the river during the Hungry Ghost Festival

Yunnan, every family would make many lotus lamps around this time, placing them at the roadside or in water so that the ghosts of wronged persons could pick them up and be reincarnated. Sunken lamps meant that ghosts must have picked them up. Some lamps were made in the shapes of birds, turtle or fish and put in the water as offerings to ghosts and spirits.

On this night, farmers in Shaanxi Province would get together to drink or hoist five-colored flags on a piece of good cropping land to symbolize harvest. In Jiangsu, people would paste colorful paper petals on the side of bowls and light the oil in the

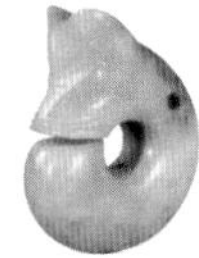

bowl, a practice known as "candle hidden in the field." In Chaoan in Guangdong, there lived a certain landlord by the name of Xu, whose bullying and oppression provoked a revolt by peasants, who killed many despotic landlords on this day. The revolt was put down. Later, on the 15th day of the seventh month, incense would be burned to commemorate those who died in the fighting.

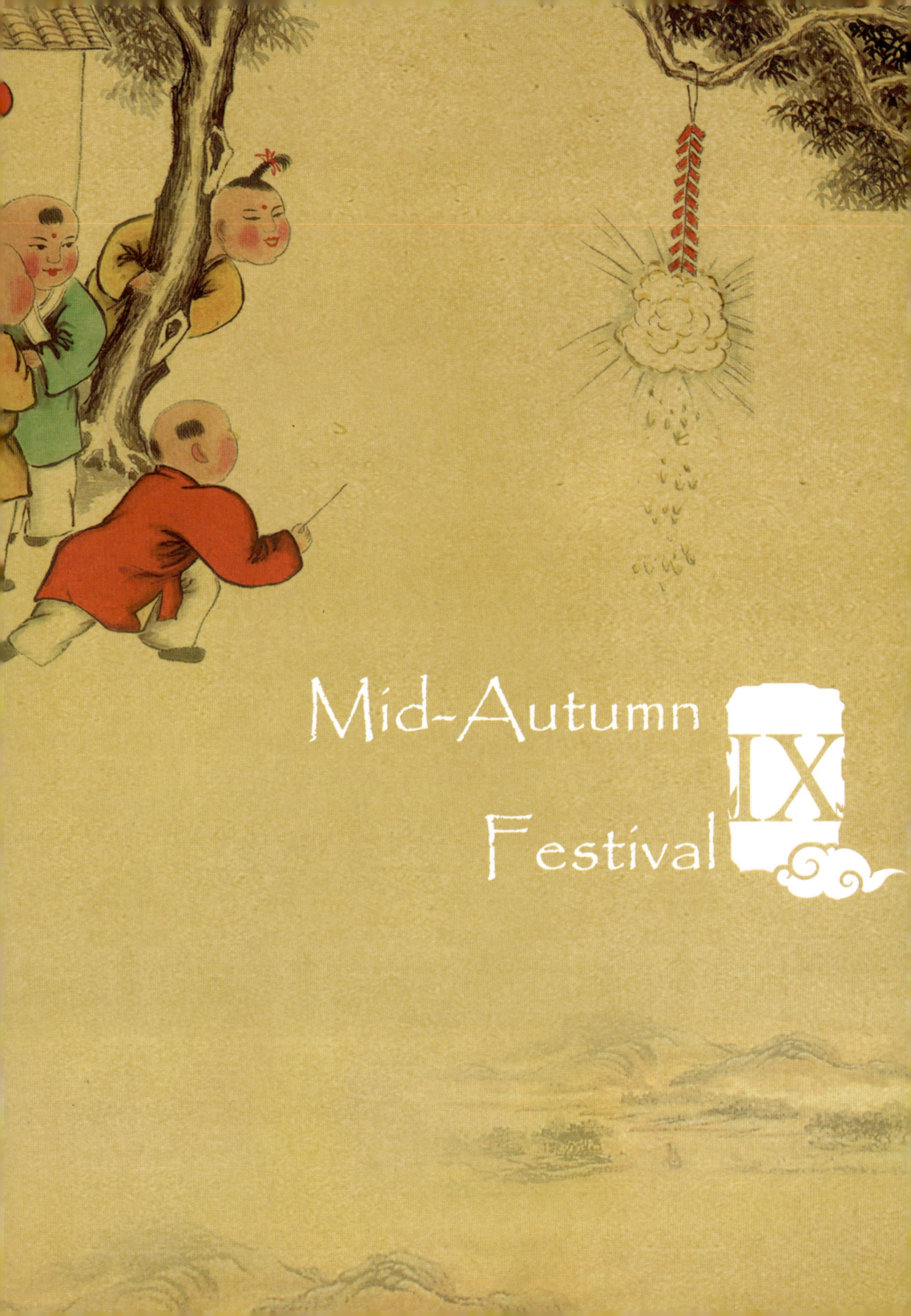
Mid-Autumn
Festival
IX

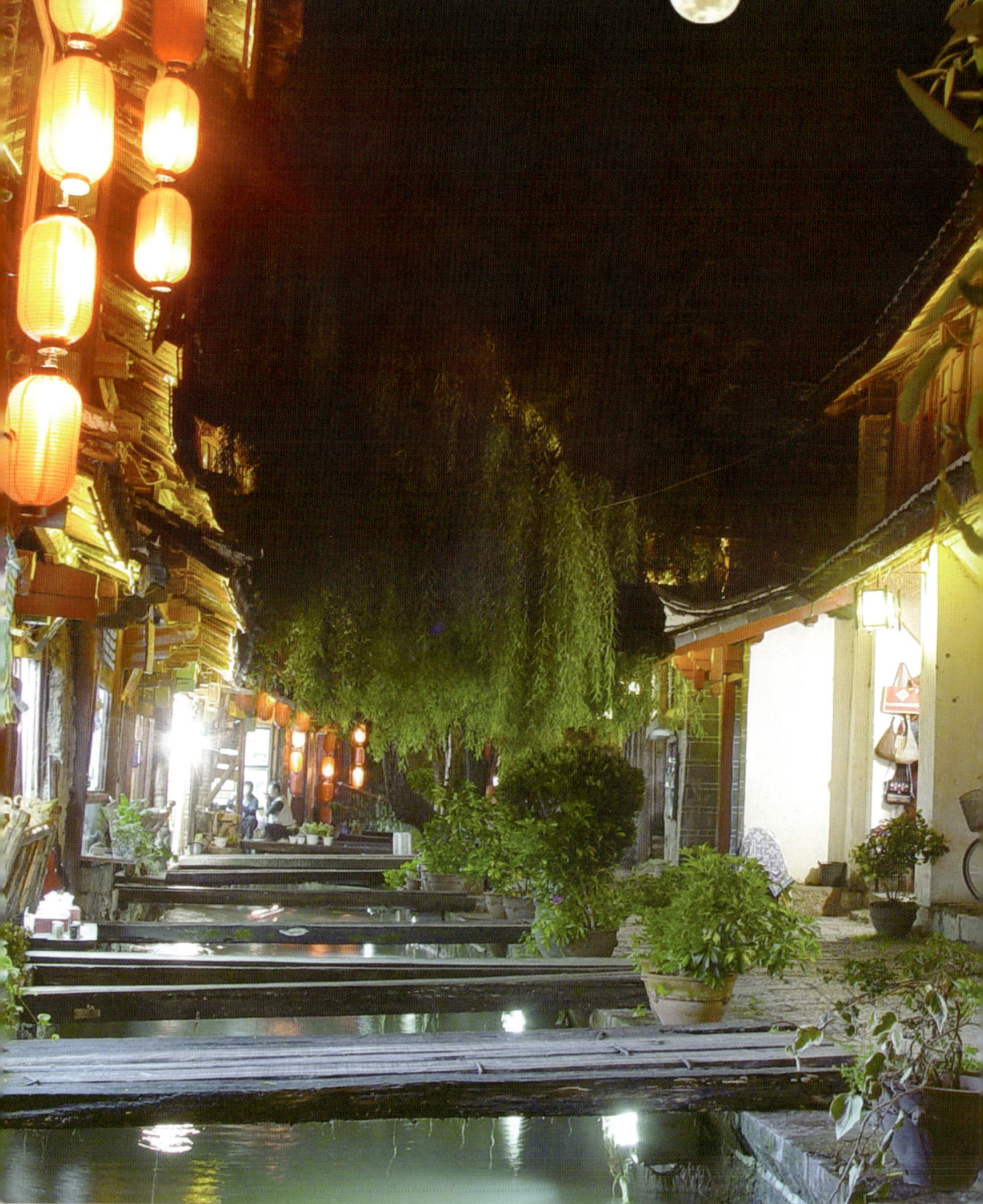

Moon-gazing during the Mid-Autumn Festival

How the Festival Got Its Name

Mid-Autumn Festival falls on the 15th day of the eighth lunar month. It was so named because the 15th day is the mid-month point, and the eighth month is the middle month of autumn, which, according to the lunar calendar, encompasses the seventh to ninth months of the year. The moon on this night is the fullest and brightest in the whole year and it also symbolizes family togetherness.

Of all the stories about the moon, that of Chang E going to the moon is the best known. Legend has it that in ancient times, there were ten suns in the sky. It was so hot that oceans boiled, mountains and earth exploded, plants were burned and people had nowhere to hide. Hou Yi, a young man good at archery, shot down nine of the suns, saving all from disaster. He became a universally loved hero. One day, on his way to visit his friend to obtain the Tao, he encountered the Queen Mother of the Western Heavens, a legendary figure of Taoist mythology who gave him a pack containing the elixir of life, which, once taken, made that person an immortal. Not wanting to leave behind his wife, Chang E, Hou Yi put the drug away rather than taking it. One day when her husband was out hunting, Chang E took the drug by mistake. Immediately, she felt as light as a cloud and flew to the sky, where a bright moon was hanging. Chang E, who had always loved to view the moon, decided to stay at the Moon Palace for a while, but once there she stayed there and never returned home. She became a fairy. In the Moon Palace lived a man by the name of Wu Gang, whose punishment was to cut down the laurel tree

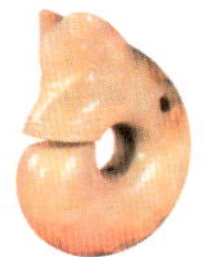

on the moon. But every time he cut into it, the cut would close immediately and the tree would never fall.

The Practice of Moon Worship

The practice of moon worship started in primitive times. On this night, tribes would light a bonfire and dance around it to celebrate a good harvest. Records show that the custom of worshipping the moon and having fun through the night started in the third century AD. Emperors of later dynasties also practiced moon worshipping on Mid-Autumn night, when music was played to pray for a good harvest.

It was with the Northern Song Dynasty that this festival came to belong to the common people. According to the *Record of the Eastern Capital*, the capital Bianliang (present-day Kaifeng) was exceptionally lively on the night of the Mid-Autumn Festival. All wine shops were decorated for the occasion and lanterns hung at stores selling vintage liquors. Fresh fruits filled the fruit shops. People would celebrate at restaurants while admiring the moon.

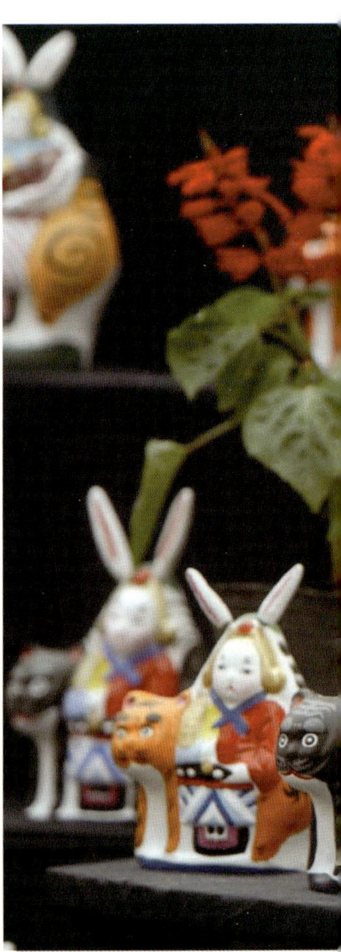

On the night of the Mid-Autumn Festival, the full moon is bright, the cool breeze refreshing and the air thick with the fragrance of sweet osmanthus. All families without exception would set up a table for incense burners under the moon. On the

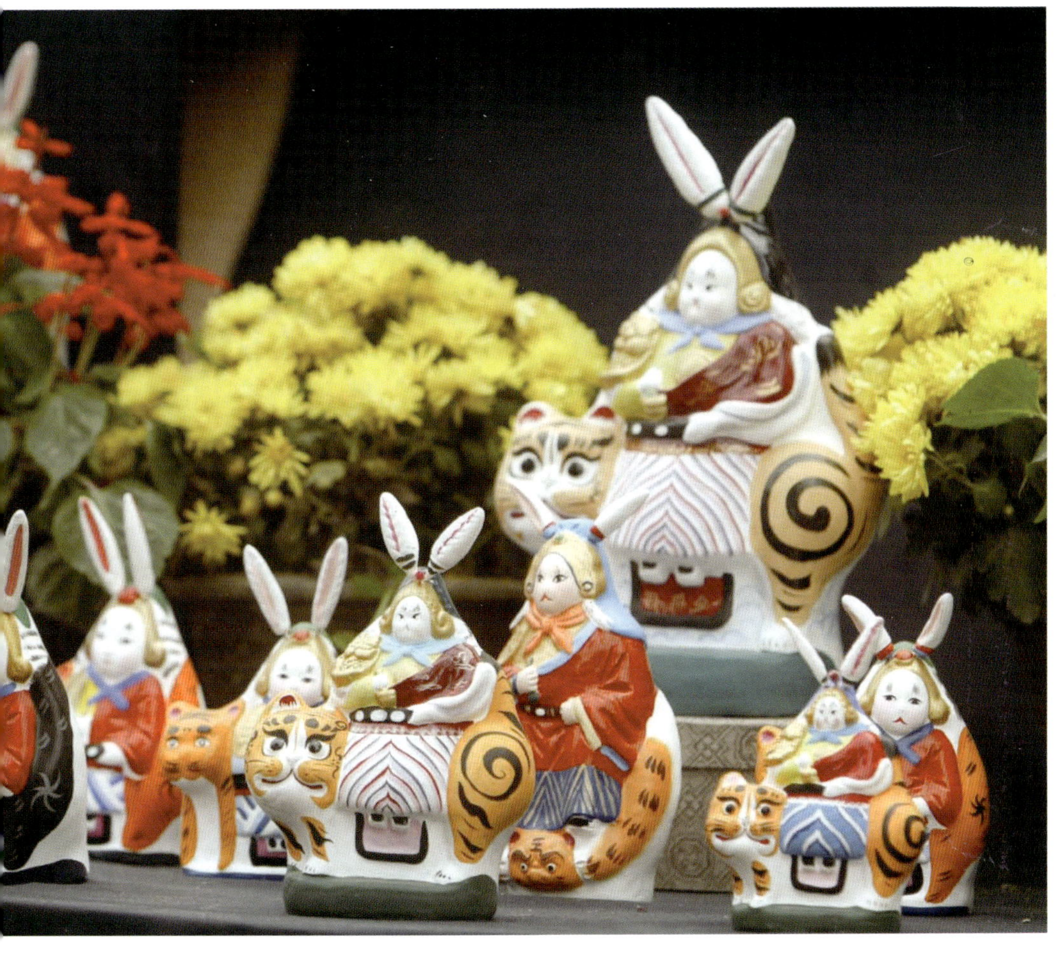

Chinese legend tells of the moon goddess Chang E, who resides in the Moon Palace with a rabbit for company, also worshipped by people during the Mid-Autumn Festival.

table would be arranged fruits in season, such as watermelon, apples, grapes, dates, pears and chestnuts; there would also be cooked soybeans, five-spice peanuts and taro. At the center of all this food was a large moon cake cut into the same number of slices as there were family members. In the incense burner, a soybean stem was planted to represent the laurel tree in the legendary Moon Palace. Then the whole family took turns to

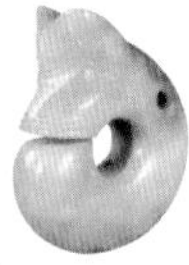

worship the moon. Once this was over, the whole family started to eat the food and chat around the table. The worshippers were generally women because the sacrifice was offered to the fairy Chang E.

Emperors of the Ming and Qing dynasties held moon worship ceremonies every year. The ceremony held by the Empress Dowager Cixi (1835-1908) was the most grand. On this night, all ministers and palace girls would gather around Cixi at the Hall of Clouds at the Summer Palace to hold the ceremony. The sacrificial food included moon cakes, seven-section lotus roots and fine fruits, as well as a specially made moon cake several foot long stamped with images of the Moon Palace, laurel tree and Chang E. There was also a large watermelon, sliced not quite all the way through, so that it opened like the petals of a lotus flower. After the moon worship, the food would be distributed among all the concubines, eunuchs, and close servant girls. Eventually, the emperor and entourage would eat a banquet aboard boats on the palace's Kunming Lake. In the meantime, they could enjoy the fireworks in the sky and the lotus lamps on the water.

The Moon Altar Park in Beijing, built in 1530, was where emperors came to worship the moon. The original main structure was an altar; other facilities included the Bell Tower, Hall for Equipment and Costumes, House of Spirits, Animal Sacrifices Pavilion and Kitchen of Peaceful Coexistence.

Moon Cake

Moon cakes are the traditional food at Mid-Autumn Festival. The shape of the cakes, perfectly round like the full moon, symbolizes reunion and reflects people's desire to be reunited.

Moon cakes originated in the Tang Dynasty and became popular during the Song. One record reads: "Moon cakes can be found everywhere, some measuring as much as one foot in diameter and bearing images of the moon palace and rabbit in the moon. Some would eat moon cakes after the ceremony; others would save it till the eve of the new year." The Song Dynasty poet Su Dongpo (1037-1101) described moon cake thus: "Chewing the moon cake is like chewing the moon; inside, all is fluffy and sweet."

In the Ming Dynasty, people gave gifts of moon cake to celebrate reunion. In the Qing Dynasty, walnuts and sugar were used as fillings, very similar to the moon cakes of today. Nowadays, there is much regional variation: Suzhou-style cakes are fluffy and use preserved fruits, bean paste and pork as filling; Beijing-style cakes look bright and have a thin crust with fillings ranging from coconut paste, lotus seed paste, date paste, nuts, candied osmanthus flowers

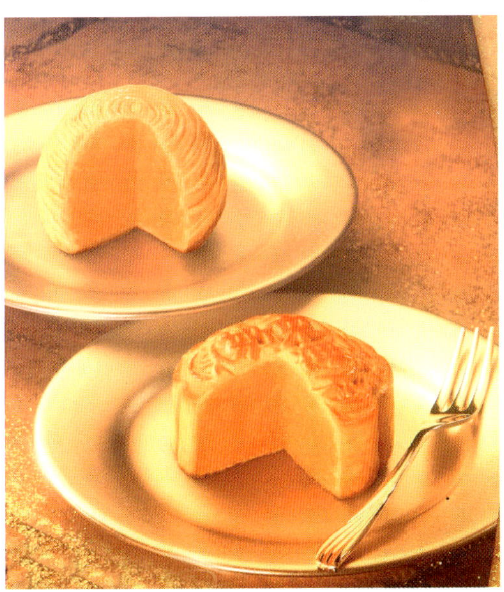

Moon cakes

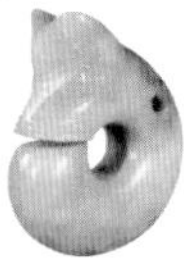

to egg yolks, chicken and ham.

Besides eating moon cakes, people in some areas have the custom of admiring osmanthus flowers, playing on swings, eating reunion dinners, drinking sweet wine, eating lotus roots and water caltrops. In other areas, people dance with lanterns and sing folk songs.

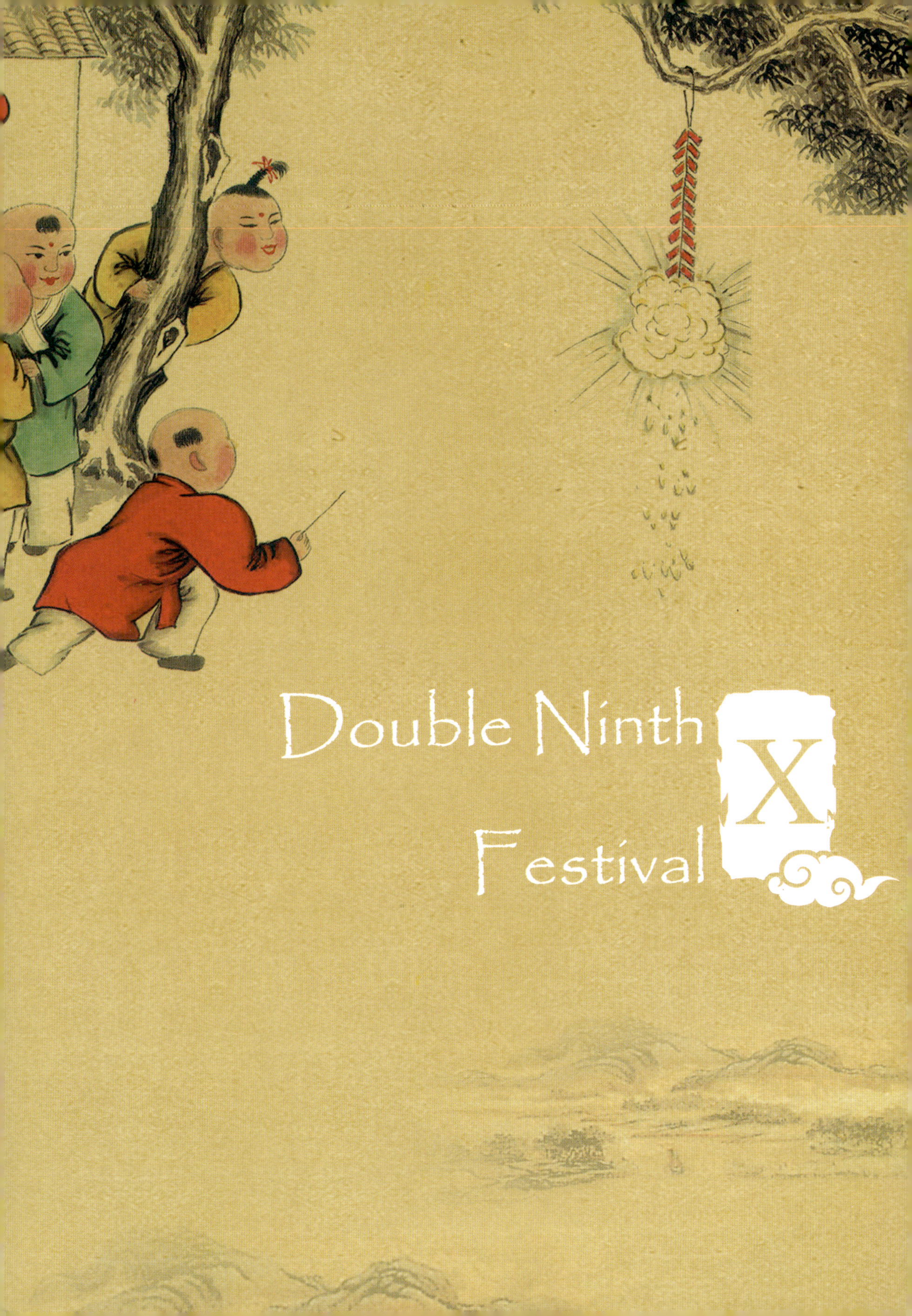

Double Ninth
Festival
X

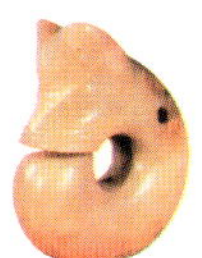

The Double Ninth Festival falls on the ninth day of the ninth lunar month. Since antiquity, people have believed that the number nine was a lucky one, symbolic of good luck, happiness and light. In Chinese, the word "99" is pronounced in the same way as the word for "everlasting." In the Forbidden City, the palace of China's Ming and Qing emperors, there were 9,999 rooms.

It was over 2,000 years ago, in the Eastern Han Dynasty, that this day became a holiday. According to

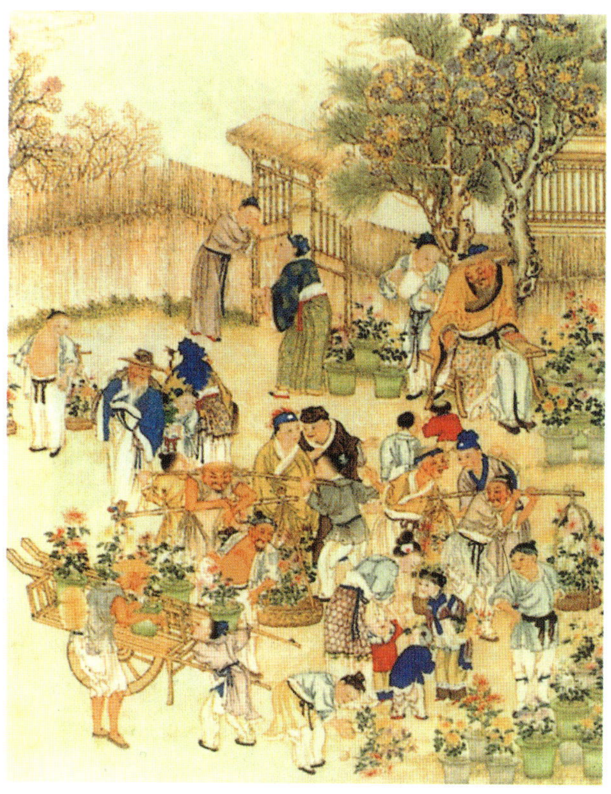

A chrysanthemum fair

historical records, a man by the name of Huan Jing acknowledged the Taoist master Fei Changfang as his teacher. One day, Fei Changfang predicted to Huan Jing that on the ninth day of the ninth month, disaster would befall Huan Jing's family and that he could only avoid the disaster by attaching a small pouch of dogwood to his arm that day, climbing to the mountain top and drinking chrysanthemum wine. Taking his teacher's advice, Huan took his family to drink chrysanthemum wine on top of a hill. They returned home to find all their livestock dead. From then on, it became a custom on this particular day to wear a small pouch on the arm and drink chrysanthemum wine on a hill.

In the Tang Dynasty, this practice became even more widespread; it was a very popular activity for friends to get together over wine and to read out their poems. Emperors of all ages participated in such festivities and many famous poems are a legacy of those days.

Customs on the Double Ninth Festival

The main custom on the Double Ninth Festival is mountain climbing, fastening dogwood to the hair, drinking chrysanthemum wine and admiring chrysanthemum flowers.

According to *Record of Customs and Habits* by Zhou Chu, "Dogwood, when pinned to the hair on the Double Ninth Day,

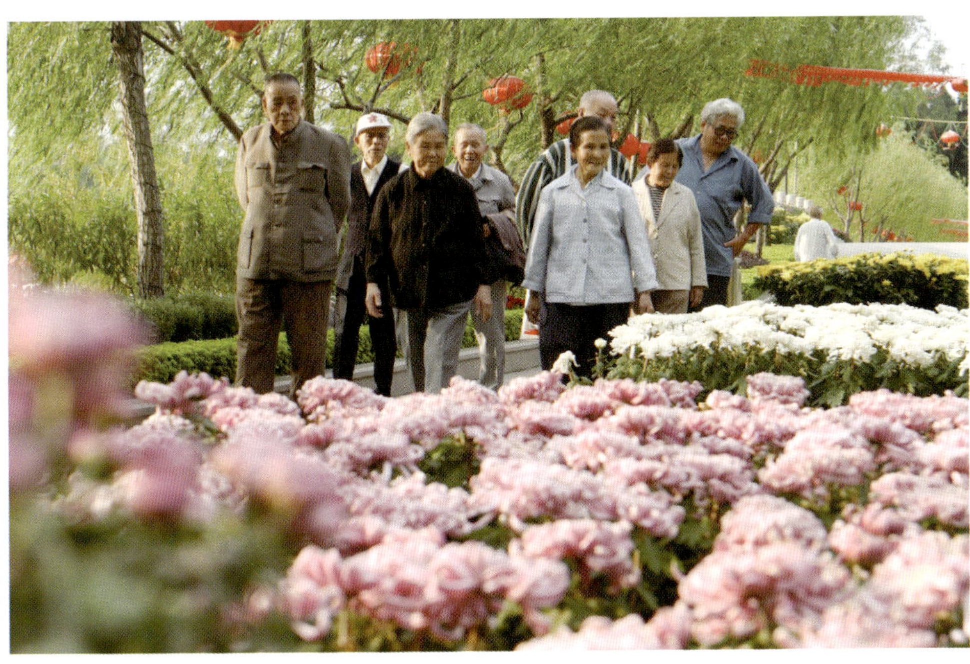

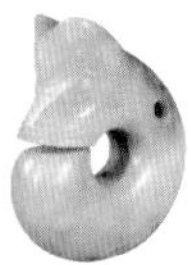

can help avoid evil spirits and early coldness." Dogwood is a small evergreen tree, which bears flowers in late spring and early summer, fruiting in the fall. Used as medicine, it has the effect of stopping pain and regulating the flow of vital energy. Its leaves can help cure cholera and its roots can kill insects. Keeping some dogwood on the person at all times can keep mosquitoes and other insects from stinging.

Admiring chrysanthemum flowers on the Double Ninth Day is a very enjoyable activity with roots back in ancient times. There are many varieties of chrysanthemum. The grand occasion of chrysanthemum viewing on the Double Ninth in the Northern Song capital was described in the *Record of the Eastern Capital*. In the Qing Dynasty, these events were held every three to five years or once every ten. But the most spectacular of all was the once-every-60-years chrysanthemum fair and those who experienced two such events in their life were counted very lucky indeed. At such fairs, poets would give readings of their work and artists would paint the flowers. Chrysanthemum fairs are still held today in some areas of China. Chrysanthemum flowers exhibited at such fairs include Chinese aster, bluish chrysanthemum, young chrysanthemum, and longevity chrysanthemum, as well as chrysanthemums used for beverages and medicine.

Drinking chrysanthemum wine is also a time-honored tradition. Chrysanthemum-steeped wine is reputed to help clear vision, cure dizziness and lower the blood pressure.

As the Double Ninth Day happens to be in the fall, it is also a good time to go mountain hiking and rowing.

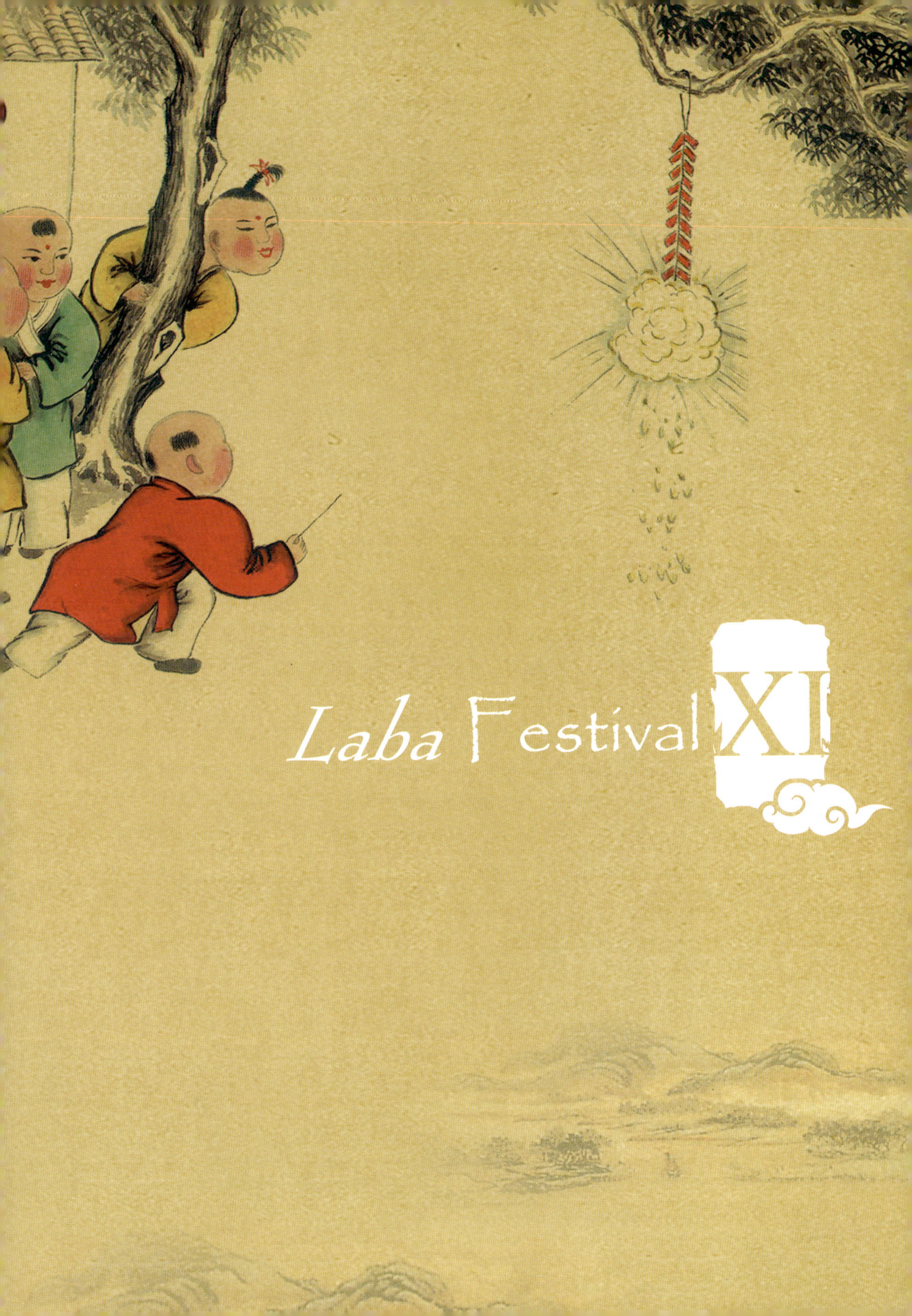
Laba Festival XI

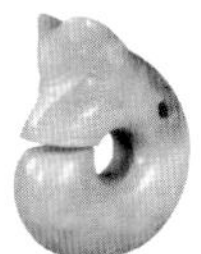

Tradition from Ancient Times

The *Laba* Festival falls on the eighth day of the twelfth lunar month. In Chinese, the twelfth lunar month is called *la*, to which is appended the word for eight (*ba*)—hence the name.

In ancient times, on *Laba* Day itself or the day before, villagers would dress up as warriors and deities of every kind and dance to beating drums, a practice they believed would help them avoid disasters and drive out evil spirits.

A Buddhist Holiday

Laba is a Buddhist holiday; the day that Han Chinese believe was the day that Sakyamuni attained the highest state of spiritual

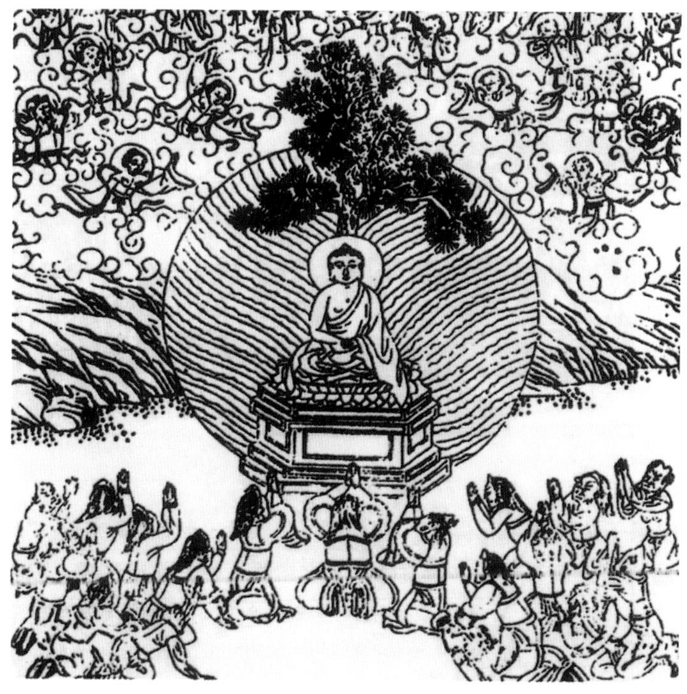

A picture of Sakyamuni becoming the Buddha

enlightenment. It was said that, prior to his enlightenment, Sakyamuni went to India to look for the truth of life. The weather was extremely hot; hungry and exhausted, he finally collapsed beside a river. When a shepherd girl happened to pass by and saw him, she fed Sakyamuni with her own lunch, which consisted of leftover sticky rice, dates, nuts and wild fruits. Sakyamuni was revitalized; he bathed in the river and then sat in meditation under a bodhi tree and attained enlightenment. This day was the eighth day of the twelfth lunar month. From then on, all monks would assemble to chant scriptures and eat sticky rice porridge in memory of Sakyamuni.

Laba Porridge

The custom of eating *Laba* porridge started in the Song Dynasty, over a thousand years ago. Not only did the imperial court, official households and monasteries eat *Laba* porridge on this occasion, the common people also started to do so. By the Qing Dynasty it was very popular. Emperors, empresses and princes would give ministers, generals as well as servant girls *Laba* porridge and distribute rice and nuts to Buddhist temples and monasteries so that their monks could eat the dish. On this day, monks would hold services of sutra chanting in memory of Sakyamuni. For the common people, preparing and eating the *Laba* porridge was their way of celebrating a good harvest.

The *Record of Yanjing*, by Fucha Dunchong of the Qing Dynasty, described the porridge thus: "Yellow rice, rice, glutinous rice, millet, water caltrop rice, chestnuts, red beans and date

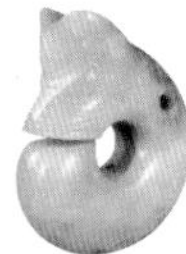

paste are mixed together and water added. Other ingredients such as walnuts, almonds, melon seeds, peanuts, hazelnuts, pine nuts, sugar and brown sugar, and raisins are added as garnish." "Preparation such as cracking nuts and washing utensils starts on the seventh day and the porridge is cooked overnight. By daybreak, it is ready. The porridge is used as sacrifice to one's ancestors and the Buddha as well as a gift to friends and family before noon."   "The porridge with more varieties is the winner." "People compete with each other to produce new varieties, which far exceed those of our ancestors." The custom of eating *Laba* porridge on the eighth day of the twelfth lunar month is still practiced today.

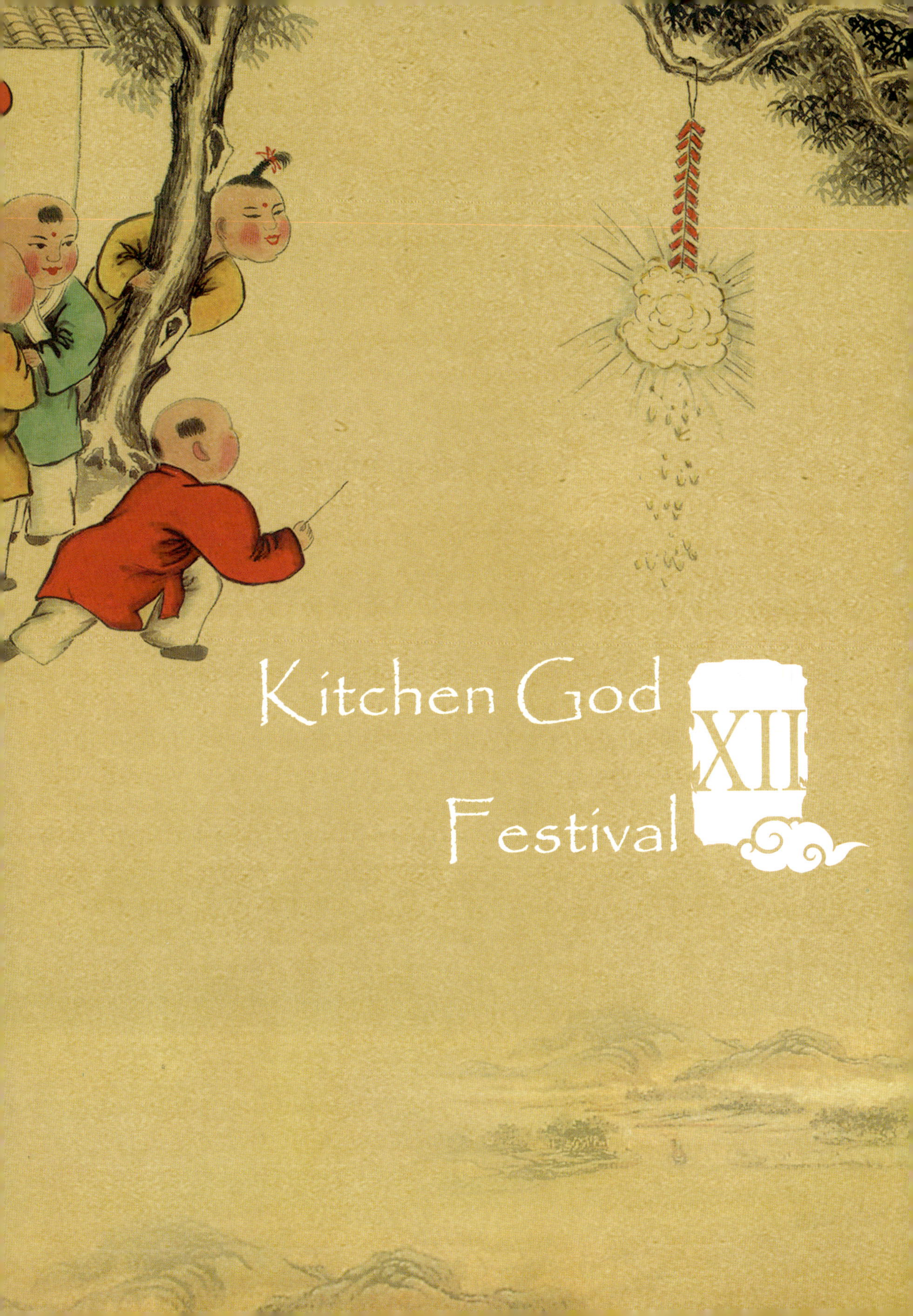

Kitchen God Festival

XII

The history of sacrificing to the Kitchen God on the 23rd day of the 12th lunar month goes back as far as three millennia.

In Chinese myth, the Kitchen God was the god in charge of kitchens on the earth and his image presided from the wall above the stove in each household. But his duties went beyond the kitchen. He was said to be the envoy sent by the Jade Emperor in heaven to record the merits and demerits of people on the earth, returning to heaven on the 23rd day of the 12th month to report to the Jade Emperor. People were afraid of offending the Kitchen God, treating him as head of their household and beseeching him to "say good things in heaven and give peace on the earth." On the 23rd day of the 12th month, the day he was supposed to report back, every household would offer sacrifices to him. Brown slab candy would be offered as sacrificial food and a straw horse would be made for the Kitchen God to ride on his way to heaven. Hay and a bowl of water would also be offered to the "horse." When everything was ready, the portrait of the Kitchen God would be taken down from the wall and burned together with all other sacrificial offerings. In this way, the Kitchen God was considered to have gone to heaven. On Chinese New Year's Eve, the day that the Kitchen God was supposed to return to the earth, a new portrait was put over the stove.

Who Was the Kitchen God?

There are many versions explaining the identity of the Kitchen God. The popular belief was that his family name was Zhang, like that of the Jade Emperor whom he served.

Regardless of his family name, the Kitchen God was a male and, this being the case, it was the male head of the household who conducted the ritual. In northern China, people believed that "men do not worship the moon and women do not sacrifice to the Kitchen God." Obviously, this practice ignored the existence of the woman next to the Kitchen God—his wife.

This is the story of the Kitchen God's wife. A long, long time ago, a young man surnamed Zhang married the beautiful and sweet Lilac. They were a hard-working couple; he tilled the land and she weaved cloth. In less than three years, the couple had accumulated a considerable amount of wealth. But before long the husband took in a concubine named Crab-apple. She was a jealous woman who was averse to working. Zhang was so besotted with her that he eventually abandoned his wife. Zhang and Crab-apple wallowed in luxury all day and soon squandered all the wealth of the family. Not caring to live in poverty, Crab-apple left Zhang and married another man. Zhang was reduced to begging. On a snowy winter day, Zhang collapsed in front of a house, suffering from cold and hunger. The maidservant of the house helped him in, and gave him a meal. Zhang was completely moved and asked her about her master. He was told that the owner of the house was a kind-hearted lady who lived by herself. As they were talking, the lady came into the room next to the

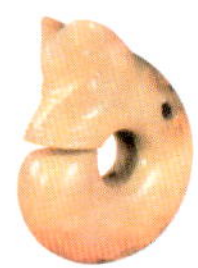

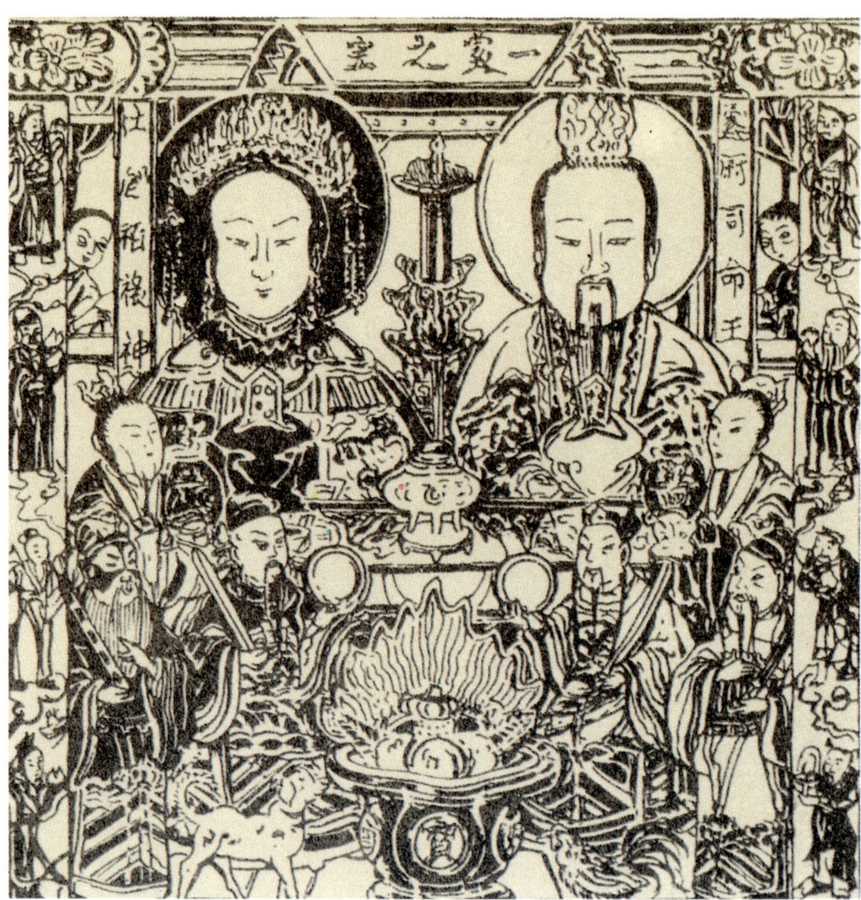

The Kitchen God and his wife

kitchen. Zhang was surprised to find that she was his former wife
Lilac. He was ashamed to meet her, and sought a place to hide. In
desperation he slipped into the stove, where he burned to death.
When Lilac realized the beggar was her former husband, she was
grief-stricken, and died a few days later.

When the Jade Emperor learnt of this, his first idea was to
penalize Zhang for leaving his wife for the younger concubine.
But he changed his mind later, considering that Zhang had
realized his error, and had paid the supreme penalty. He bestowed
the title Kitchen God on Zhang and Kitchen God's Wife on Lilac,
and let people worship them in their kitchens.

Kitchen God Sacrifice Customs

Despite some three thousand years of the practice, sacrifices
to the Kitchen God were not elaborate affairs. In the words of
the Tang poet Luo Yin, "A cup of tea and a wisp of smoke send
the Kitchen God to heaven." Clearly, in the Tang Dynasty, the
offerings were no more than a cup of tea and a stick of incense.
Later people feared that such meager offerings might offend this
heavenly god, and, for want of a better idea, they started to offer

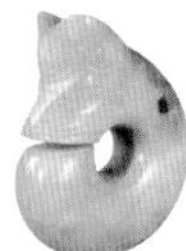

brown slab candy to the Kitchen God, it being very sticky and able, hopefully, to seal his lips when he went to report to the Jade Emperor.

The custom of offering sacrifices to the Kitchen God is still practiced today on the 23rd day of the 12th lunar month. But today it is children who are given the sticky offerings rather than the Kitchen God.

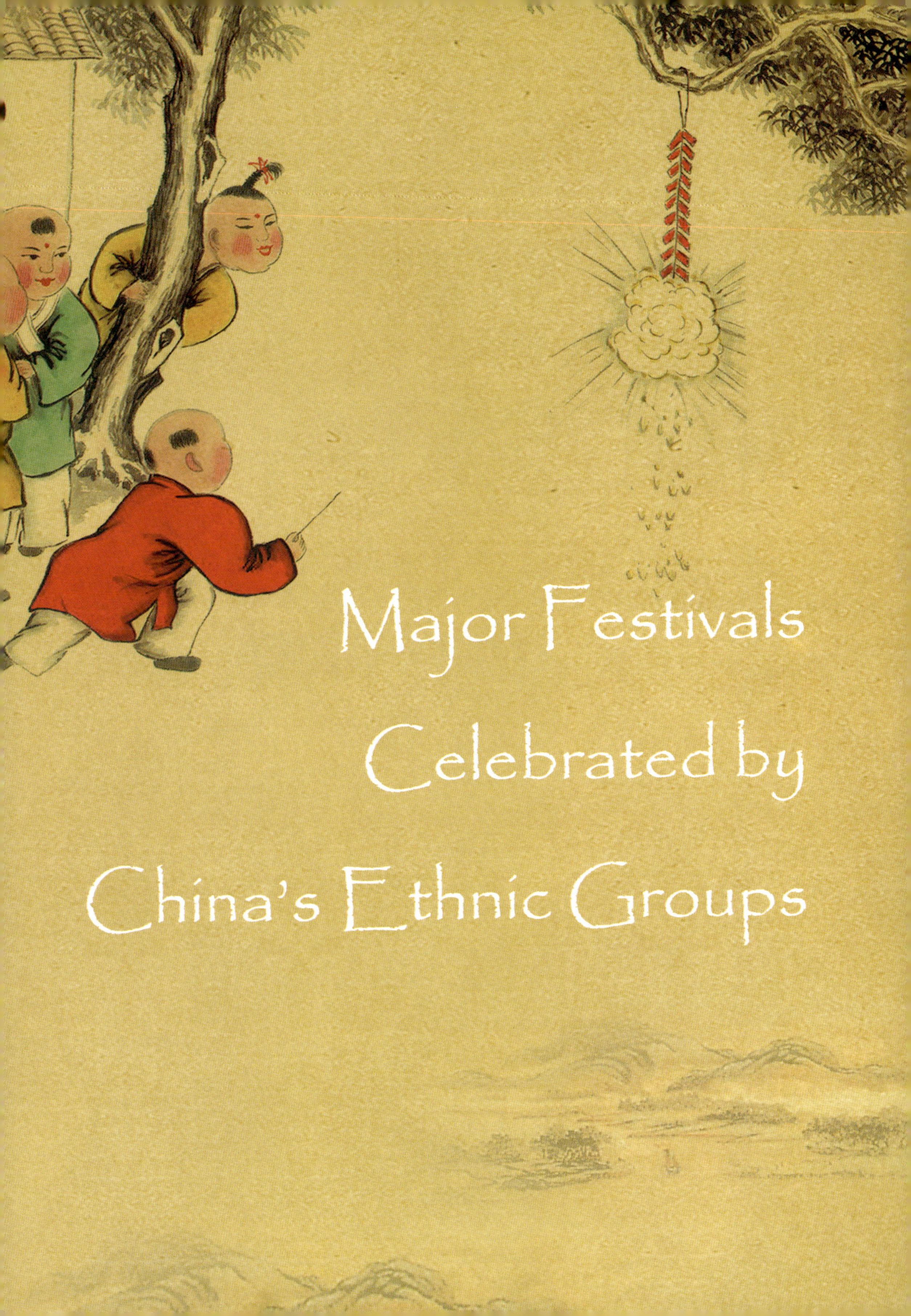

Major Festivals
Celebrated by
China's Ethnic Groups

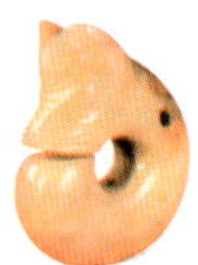

Tibetan New Year

According to the Tibetan calendar, there are twelve months in a year. The solar month consists of 30 days and the lunar month, 29 days. So as to align the months with the seasons, a leap month is added once every two and a half to three years. Generally speaking, Tibetan New Year arrives soon after the Chinese New Year.

Tibetan New Year is the most important holiday in Tibet but it is celebrated on different dates in different areas. In Lhasa, it is celebrated on the 1st day of the 1st Tibetan month; south of the Nyangchu River, it falls on the 1st day of the 12th Tibetan month;; and in some areas in Qamdo, it is on the 1st day of the 11th Tibetan month. As Tibetans are Buddhists, their New Year celebrations are full of religious sanctity.

Bathing Festival in Tibet

The Bathing Festival falls around the end of summer and beginning of fall, from the night that the planet Venus appears in the night sky until it disappears a week later. Tibetans have been celebrating this festival for seven or eight hundred years. During the festival, irrespective of age or gender, all wash themselves and their garments in rivers and lakes. Thousands of people come to the Lhasa River to celebrate the holiday. The drinking of barley wine and butter tea generally follows.

Firework Festival of the Dong People

The Firework Festival or Firework Fair is a major traditional holiday celebrated by the Dong people and falls on the third day of the third lunar month. The most representative is that celebrated at Fulu Town, in the Sanjiang Dong Autonomous County of Guangxi.

The fireworks are divided into three types known as first gun (symbolizing a large family), fortune gun (for prosperity) and noble gun (meaning career promotion). Each is tied with a metal ring, a symbol of happiness, and wrapped with red and green thread. They are then put into the cannon. When lit, the metal ring flies into the sky. As it falls people scramble to catch it. Whoever catches the metal ring first and takes it to a command post is the winner.

Water Splashing Festival of the Dai People

The Water Splashing Festival is celebrated in southwest China by the Bulang, De'ang and Achang ethnic groups, who all use the Dai calendar. But the Water Splashing Festival celebrated by the Dai minority is that group's most popular and important holiday. The festival, which started some 700 years ago, falls on the New Year of the Dai people. It starts around April 11 each year and lasts about four days, the first two spent sending off the old year and the last two devoted to welcoming in the new.

During the festival, people go to the temple to bathe the Buddha before they can splash water on each other. When

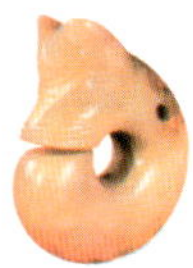

the splashing gets underway, girls generally carry a bucket of fragranced cold water, using a sprig to sprinkle water onto elders and guests to express their blessing. The climax of the festival comes when people start dousing water over each other, conveying their good luck wishes.

The Third Month Street Fair

This annual goods trading fair of the Bai people is held in Dali in Yunnan Province from the 10th to the 21st day of the third lunar month.

Third Month Street is also called Guanyin City, after the Buddhist goddess of mercy. Legend has it that a long, long time ago, Guanyin came to Dali to spread the Buddhist scriptures on the 15th day of the third month. After that, people would worship Buddha, chant scriptures and offer sacrifices on that anniversary, and the event became a temple fair. Since Dali was also a transport hub and ancient Yunnan had a large Buddhist population, the fair gradually became a trading market. The traditional Third Month Street Fair includes the trading of supplies such as mules, horses, mountain products, herbs and tea. Other activities include antiphonal singing between a man and a woman and dancing among the Bai. The Yi, Bai, Hui and Tibetan people engage in horse racing and singing.

Danu Festival of the Yao People

In the language of the Yao minority, "Danu" means forget not. The major holiday of the Yao people in Guangxi, this is the day to worship Miluotuo, the first ancestor of the Yao people. The festival falls on the 29th day of the fifth lunar month. Depending on regional customs and the farming season, this festival is observed at different intervals—once every two or three years in some areas, every three to five in others. In some places, it is once every 12 or 13 years.

Before the festival, every family undertakes a thorough cleaning and preparation for the festival dinner such as making rice wine and rice cake. Festival activities include singing and dancing, martial arts and ball games. The bronze drum dance is the most eye-catching of all.

Torch Festival of the Yi People

The Torch Festival, which falls on the 24th day of the sixth lunar month, is the grandest holiday of the Yi people in Liangshan, Sichuan Province. Every household drinks and eats meat and kills animals as sacrifice to their ancestors. The men, dressed in their festival finery, participate in bull, goat and cock fighting, horse racing and wrestling while women sing songs, play the mouth organ and the *yueqin* mandolin. In the evening, people hold torches and walk around their houses. On the third night, groups of people walk into the fields and mountains carrying torches before gathering at one spot to make a bonfire. They then drink, sing and dance by the fire until daybreak.

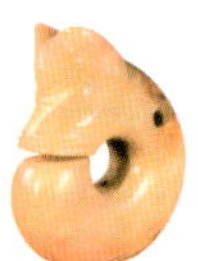

Autumn Festival of the Miao People

The Autumn Festival, celebrated on the first day of autumn, or one or two days after, is the most important festival of the Miao people in western Hunan Province. On the morning of the festival, farmers stop farm work, put on their holiday best and set up a stage in the field to hold a singing and drum dance contest. After this event, two respected elders are elected to dress up as the "old men of autumn," who give good wishes for the harvest and happiness to everyone.

Mongolian Nadam Fair

Nadam means entertainment and games in Mongolian. The traditional Nadam fair, a cultural and sports fair to celebrate a successful year, is held in August every year.

On this day, everyone wears their holiday best to watch or participate in horse racing, wrestling, archery, singing and dancing. Nadam is also a commodity fair trading in agricultural and livestock supplies. In addition to industrial and agricultural products local foods such as beef, lamb, smoked foods, butter and cream are also traded.

'Id al-Kurban Festival

A Muslim holiday, *'Id al-Kurban* Festival is celebrated by the Hui, Uighur, Kazak, Uzbek, Tajik, Tatar, Kirgiz, Salar, Dongxiang and Bonan ethnic groups. It is also known as "festival of slaughtering animals."

'Id al-Kurban Festival falls on the 10th day of the 12th lunar month. Before the festival, every household cleans their house and prepares festival food. On the early morning of the festival, Muslims bathe, burn incense and dress formally to attend a service at the mosque. On this day, Uighurs in cities and countryside in northwestern China's Xinjiang hold grand singing and dancing parties outdoors.

Festival of Fast Breaking

The ninth month of the Islamic calendar is Ramadan, the month of fasting, during which the faithful may not drink, eat or have sex between dawn and sunset. It is meant to make people reflect on their sins and make the rich empathize with the feelings of hunger and suffering. The fast ends on the first day of the 10th Islam month, when the fast breaking is celebrated.

On this day, people rise early, take a bath and burn incense before attending service at the mosque. This is followed by visiting the cemetery to pay respects to the dead. Also on this day, people greet each other in their neighborhood. Every household also makes deep fried food and entertains friends and family with beef and lamb.

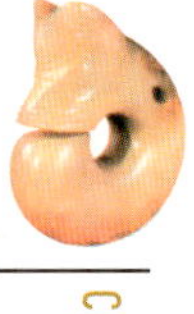

Duan Festival of the Shui People

Also known as the Melon Festival, the *Duan* Festival is the beginning of the New Year according to the traditional calendar of the Shui people in southwest China. It is the longest holiday in the world, lasting 49 days from the eighth to the 10th lunar month.

During the holiday, the Shui engage in dancing and singing. Visitors can see the ancient and mysterious Shui script and horse tail embroidery, and to watch folk performances such as fire dragon dance, water dragon play, duck snatching and horse racing. At the same time, visitors can also get a glimpse of the solemn ceremony of offering ancestral sacrifices.

The Singing Fair of the Zhuang People

The Zhuang people are known for their good singing voices. The annual Singing Fair, also known as the Third Day of the Third Month Festival, is the grandest of all the Zhuang singing fairs.

On this day, five-color steamed rice and colorful eggs are served. The fair, held on a ground not far from the village, lasts for two or three days and may have anything from one or two thousand participants to tens of thousands. At the singing fair, single men and women sing in antiphonal style. Through their singing, they decide whether they like each other and, if so, exchange tokens as a pledge of their engagement. Other activities include tossing a colored silk ball or egg, generally by a woman to the man she likes as a pledge of love. It is also a way of having fun.

Kazak Ballad Singers' Fair

Kazak balladeers are folk song artists who, besides singing, can all play stringed instruments and improvise songs and poems, even memorize many epics. The Kazak Ballad Singers' Fair is generally held on the grasslands, lasting for a week or a fortnight and attracting herders from far and near. Here balladeers of all ages sing and read poems in antiphonal style. Sometimes, the fair becomes so competitive it carries on through the night.

Singing and Dancing Fair of the Jingpo People

The largest singing fair of the Jingpo people in Yunnan, this is held on the 15th or 16th day of the first lunar month.

The fair is held on a square, in the center of which are set up four totem poles painted with the sun, mountains and winding roads. The Jingpo people believe they are the descendents of the God of Sun from the far-away Tibetan Plateau, and the winding roads symbolize the long and arduous migration of their ancestors. Under the direction of a lead dancer—the men waving broadswords, the women waving handkerchiefs and colorful fans—the dancers create a magnificent spectacle with their vigorous steps and constantly changing formations.

图书在版编目（CIP）数据

中国节：英文 / 齐星编 . 妙龄译 .
—北京：外文出版社，2008
ISBN 978-7-119-05407-0
I. 中 ... II. ①齐 ... ②妙 ... III. 节日—风俗习惯
—中国—英文 IV. K892.1

中国版本图书馆 CIP 数据核字（2008）第 088347 号

英文翻译：妙　龄
英文审定：Sue Duncan　贺　军
责任编辑：刘芳念
装帧设计：华审书装
印刷监制：韩少乙

中国节

作　　者：齐　星
图片提供：刘　臣　CFP

© 2008 外文出版社
出版发行：
外文出版社出版（中国北京百万庄大街24号）
邮政编码：100037
网　　址：**www.flp.com.cn**
电　　话：008610-68320579（总编室）
　　　　　008610-68995852（发行部）
　　　　　008610-68327750（版权部）
印　　刷：
北京外文印刷厂

开本：787mm×1092mm　1/16　　印张：7
2008年第1版第1次印刷
（英）
ISBN 978-7-119-05407-0
07800（平）
85-E-637 P